Praise for *The Key to Everything*

From Corporate America

The Key to Everything reads like a conversation with a friend, which allows the crossover to trust and a mind-set of receptivity. Matt displays a heartfelt concern for you to accomplish success, but more importantly, he gives you the tools with which to accomplish it.

> Bert Lindsay, dealer principal, Lindsay Honda/Acura, Columbus, OH

The teachings in this book will help you unlock your teachability and will help the leaders you work with become more teachable.

> Michael R. Lover, zone leader, 7-Eleven, Inc.

When I first started reading this book I patted myself on the back and looked forward to passing it along to all of the unteachable people in my life. However, by the middle of the book, I was looking in the mirror and evaluating the ways I could improve. Amazing! My teachability index started rising while I was reading the book.

> Rhonda Williams, manager, creative services, Hertz, Inc.

Matt addresses how a lack of teachability will hold you back and then shows you how to conquer it. Get ready; *The Key to Everything* will change your life!

> Kirby Cameron, senior PC commercial representative, The Sherwin-Williams Company, North America's largest coatings manufacturer

The Key to Everything is the start of a journey of self-awareness. Allow yourself to be inspired by its strategies to pursue your full potential.

> William Smith, GSM Scanlon, Lexus, Fort Myers, FL

The Key to Everything breathes a fresh approach to tackling age-old performance issues that torment our organizations, leaders, and ourselves. Matt's personality shines through as he infuses his easy-to-read chapters with bursts of practical wisdom and unique style, making this book an exceptionally rare find.

KIM WILSON, ORGANIZATIONAL LEARNING
SPECIALIST, WALGREEN CO., SW FLORIDA

FROM MOTIVATIONAL SPEAKERS
AND LEADERSHIP EXPERTS

Matt Keller has a remarkable ability to connect biblical principles to our modern day lives. In this inspiring read, Matt reveals the one thing that every great leader has in common--read it and discover the key to changing your life.

RORY VADEN, COFOUNDER, SOUTHWESTERN CONSULTING;
NEW YORK TIMES BESTSELLING AUTHOR, *TAKE THE STAIRS*

The Key to Everything is an essential read for anyone wanting to maintain a trajectory of growth in life and work.

TODD HENRY, AUTHOR, *LOUDER THAN WORDS* AND *DIE EMPTY*

This is a book that you will not be able to put down. The ideas and strategies are life changing. The teachability formula will release fresh creativity and success in every area or your life.

BOB HARRISON, DR INCREASE

FROM THE CHURCH WORLD

After spending time with Matt over the past three years I have learned that teachability is the key to his success. This book will not only unlock doors to your organization's growth, but it will also show you the key to growing personally. Matt's humor and practicality in this book make it a must-read for you and the team you lead.

KEVIN MYERS, AUTHOR, *HOME RUN*; LEAD
PASTOR, 12STONE CHURCH

Matt Keller has done it again. He has written a book we all need to read. Matt's life embodies this message and it shows as each page is full of personal revelation and insight that will empower all of us to live more teachable lives.

Pastor Brady Boyd, New Life Church, Colorado Springs; author, *Addicted to Busy*

In *The Key to Everything*, Matt gives readers a practical approach to getting past roadblocks in life as well as how to grow after them. With a desire to learn, and a willingness to grow, this book can change your life!

Pastor Rob Ketterling, lead pastor, River Valley Church; author, *Thrill Sequence* and *Change Before You Have To*

In *The Key to Everything* Matt Keller presents a blueprint for living a happy, fulfilled life that welcomes change with open arms. Through sound biblical principles and candid personal reflection, he develops the idea of teachability as the secret to physical, spiritual, and mental growth. This book so expertly shows the reader how to avoid the pitfalls of fear and insecurity, instead offering a path of discovery and renewed focus.

Matthew Barnett, senior pastor, Angelus Temple & Co; founder, The Dream Center

We all want to be successful in what we do but we aren't always sure what it will take to get there. No matter who we are or what we are doing, there is one thing that is necessary in everything we do: teachability. In Matt's book, you'll learn about what it means to be teachable, and how understanding the DNA of teachability can change everything.

Greg Surratt, founding and lead pastor, Seacoast Church; president, Association of Related Church's (ARC)

Matt is such a wise, life-giving pastor and friend. I believe everyone can learn from the lessons and challenges found in *The Key to Everything*. I encourage you to really take time to sift through the roadblocks to teachability and understand what characteristics you must embrace to be teachable like Matt.

Todd Mullins, lead pastor, Christ Fellowship

FROM THE GOVERNMENT/PUBLIC SERVICE SECTOR

If you are interested in a recipe for quality of life *The Key to Everything* offers you a path.

RANDALL P. HENDERSON JR., MAYOR, FORT MYERS, FLORIDA

Matt's perspective and illustrations on the characteristics of teachability hit home. Becoming flexible and open to receiving feedback is not a sign of weakness, as I once perceived. It is strategic in gaining awareness and fresh insight.

COLONEL THOMAS EBERHARDT, CJM, LEE COUNTY SHERIFF'S OFFICE

FROM THE NONPROFIT WORLD

If people can increase their teachability they can vastly increase their worth at any organization, especially in today's dynamic environment. Matt sets out a digestible framework to do just that.

KATHERINE C. GREEN, PRESIDENT/CEO, HABITAT FOR
HUMANITY OF LEE AND HENDRY COUNTIES, INC.

The Key to Everything

The Key to

EVERYTHING

*Unlocking the Secret to Why Some
People Succeed and Others Don't*

MATT KELLER

NELSON
BOOKS
An Imprint of Thomas Nelson

Published in Nashville, Tennessee, by Nelson Books, an imprint of Thomas Nelson. Nelson Books and Thomas Nelson are registered trademarks of HarperCollins Christian Publishing, Inc.

Thomas Nelson, Inc., titles may be purchased in bulk for educational, business, fund-raising, or sales promotional use. For information, please e-mail SpecialMarkets@ ThomasNelson.com.

Unless otherwise noted, Scripture quotations are taken from the Holy Bible, New International Version®, NIV®. Copyright © 1973, 1978, 1984, 2011 by Biblica, Inc.™ Used by permission of Zondervan. All rights reserved worldwide. www.zondervan.com. Scripture quotations marked NLT are from *Holy Bible*, New Living Translation. © 1996, 2004, 2007. Used by permission of Tyndale House Publishers, Inc., Wheaton, Illinois 60189. All rights reserved. Scripture quotation marked ESV is from THE ENGLISH STANDARD VERSION. © 2001 by Crossway Bibles, a division of Good News Publishers. Scripture quotation marked HCSB is from the HOLMAN CHRISTIAN STANDARD BIBLE. © 1999, 2000, 2002, 2003 by Broadman and Holman Publishers. All rights reserved. Scripture quotation marked ASV is from the American Standard Version of the Bible.

ISBN-13: 978-0-7180-7806-5 (IE)

Library of Congress Control Number: 2015935256

ISBN-13: 978-1-4002-0498-4

Printed in the United States of America

15 16 17 18 19 RRD 6 5 4 3 2 1

To Jo Keller
You taught me how to love learning
Even when it meant taking us all over the country to do it!
I love you, Mom

With one day's reading a man may have the key in his hands.

—EZRA POUND

Contents

—

Preface

—

Who Do I Think I Am?

I know what you're thinking right now.

At least I think I do.

You've just picked up this book and looked at the title. And you're thinking: *Really? Considering the hundreds of thousands of books that have been written since books were invented, does this guy honestly claim to offer the one principle that can change everything for me? The Key to Everything? Does he have any idea how arrogant that sounds?*

I do.

I hear you.

And I'll admit it does sound arrogant.

In fact, I've been in that skeptical place myself—and not only about writing this book. I, too, have stood over a table at a bookstore, looked at a title, and questioned what it claimed. I've thought the same thing about samples I've downloaded on my iPad, only to be less than convinced by what I read.

So, yes, I recognize that making a claim as big as I am making sounds a bit ridiculous. I recognize I am setting myself up for the classic overpromise-underdeliver thing. And I recognize that I may have just given you every reason to shut this book or delete the sample on your eReader right now.

But I'm willing to take that chance.

I'm willing to go all the way out on this limb, make this claim, and try with all my might to convince you to hear me out.[1]

I Don't Know You, but I Know Something About You

If there's one thing I know about you, it is that you want to succeed. Deep inside all human beings is the desire to improve their lives and make the world better. You are no different. Whatever you are setting your mind to, whatever you're pointing your life at, whatever goals you're working toward or dreams you have in your heart, I know you want to succeed. We all share that fact in common.

But simply wanting to succeed isn't enough, especially these days.

Because the world has changed—and not just in a "My kids don't call me anymore, all they want to do is text" kind of way (although that may be true).

While we have been careening through the technology revolution, there has also been a shift in how we humans interact, and that shift has impacted everything about our lives. The rules of the game have changed. Consequently, the way we get to success in our lives has changed as well.

Did you get that? *In today's world the desire to be successful has not changed. But how we get there has.*

Success no longer automatically comes to the one who works the most or tries the hardest. Success no longer hinges on who you know, what you do, or where you come from. The game has changed, and the doorway to success in your world today is predicated on one single thing. One key holds the power to unlock the success you desire in your life. In whatever way you desire to be successful, there is one element that matters more than all the rest.

IN TODAY'S WORLD THE DESIRE TO BE SUCCESSFUL HAS NOT CHANGED. BUT HOW WE GET THERE HAS.

But here's the funny thing. This element isn't laid out in most job orientations. It doesn't live in the mission statement on the wall of your place of employment, and it didn't come in the owner's manual you got when you left the hospital with your first kid.[2] It's not on the front page of many corporate websites, and it certainly wasn't in your marriage vows on your wedding day. But this one principle is the key to success in all of those areas I just mentioned.

THE ONE THING THAT'S MISSING

Now don't hear what I'm not saying. It's not that all the things that used to be linked to success—hard work, discipline, grit, willpower, determination, perseverance, even chance—don't matter any longer.

They do.

They just don't matter *first*.

Before all of those things come into play as factors to our success, something else matters first.

And that's *teachability*.

Even as I type this into my computer, my word-processing app doesn't recognize the word *teachability*. It's got it underlined in bright red as if to say, "What the heck do you mean by that?" I actually had to add the word *teachability* to the dictionary of my computer to make that little red line go away.[3]

Perhaps the lack of *teachability* on my computer is indicative of the greater point I'm trying to make. We live in a world that lacks the one thing it needs in order to be successful. We live in a world that has failed to add *teachability* to its lexicon. And therein lies the problem, not just with our world in general, but with so many of the people who are striving to succeed within it. Because teachability truly is the key to everything!

Now, here's where your skepticism might kick in again.

Really Matt, you're trying to tell me that some word you apparently made up determines whether I succeed or fail?[4]

Well, I didn't make the word up. It's been around a long time, and thought leaders like John Maxwell, Seth Godin, and Roger Seip have begun to popularize the term more and more in the last decade or so. Our world just doesn't recognize its power quite yet.

But yes, I wholeheartedly believe that *teachability* describes the difference between those who succeed and those who do not in today's world. Because of the increasing rate of speed at which our world is moving today and the overwhelming volume of change happening on a daily basis, teachability will be the only way for you to succeed in the next half century. It's as if our world is a moving walkway, like at the airport, and the minute we step off and stop moving, growing, learning, and adapting with it, we are going to be left behind.

Right now there are people around you who are well-educated, creative, hardworking, and crazy talented. But without teachability, their ability to go where they want to go in life will be limited. Hard work will only take a person so far. The same is true of talent, creativity, and the right connections.

Without teachability there is a better-than-good chance that they will never see their dreams come true. Without teachability you and I will never reach our full potential or leave a mark on the world as we all desire to do.

A LACK OF TEACHABILITY WILL HOLD YOU BACK

I see so many people, young and old, who have so much potential but aren't living up to it because of their lack of teachability. A year or so ago, I was talking to one of my wife, Sarah's, friends about a dating relationship that had suddenly ended. When I asked her why she had broken things off with her boyfriend, she said, "He just wasn't teachable."

Those four words told me everything I needed to know. Sarah's friend understood that a lack of teachability would quickly put the lid on her relationship. Ending it sooner than later was the best decision she could have made.

About six months ago Sarah and I were out to dinner with a

couple who had recently had a baby. Over dinner the struggling new mom began to open up about the difficulties she was facing with her newborn. My wife listened carefully. Then she asked some questions and offered a few suggestions for how the young mother could approach some of these challenges. But the young mother immediately threw up a defensive wall and refused to be open to anything my wife was trying to say. Of course, as this was happening, the poor husband was locking eyes with me as if to say, *I don't know why she won't listen right now.* I could tell he was desperate for his wife to hear what Sarah was saying, but he lacked the ability to get his wife to embrace teachability in that moment.

One final illustration of the importance of teachability is in our work with leaders. Each year we work with hundreds of leaders who are in the entrepreneurial start-up phases of their organizations. As we are getting to know these new leaders and assessing them, it doesn't take long to identify the ones who possess teachability and the ones who don't. We have learned that people's level of teachability is the greatest determinant of their long-term success. And interestingly, we can usually detect their level of teachability in less than fifteen minutes.

Teachability matters in every area of life, from career advancement, to our dating relationships, to marriage, to how we raise our kids. It breaks my heart to see so many people with so much of the right stuff lack the one thing that could set them on their path to success and keep them going.

Teachability is the new key to everything in life.

The person who taps into the power of teachability is the person who wins. The person who grabs hold of teachability is the one who becomes great. No matter what they want, where they want to go, or what dream they have for their future, the people with the most teachability will have the most success in life.

And here's the best news: teachability is for everybody. It's not an inborn talent or knack granted only to a few. Every person on planet earth has the potential to develop a lifestyle of teachability. It is a choice and a learned trait. Which means teachability is available to you.

A LITTLE ABOUT ME AND A DISCLAIMER

Before we go any further, let me tell you a little about myself.

I have spent the last twenty years of my life working with people, and I have seen this teachability thing up close and personal. I am privileged to pastor a great church in Fort Myers, Florida, called Next Level Church, which has grown from a handful of us in a coffee shop in 2002 to nearly four thousand people now in weekly attendance. Obviously, working in such a setting gives me a lot of opportunities to see the effects of teachability on a daily basis.

Personally speaking, teachability has been a defining characteristic of my life. In other words, I love to learn. Since I was a teenager I have had this teachability thing going on, and I didn't even really know what I had. But as I've already mentioned, teachability isn't something that some people are born with and others aren't. Teachability is a characteristic that can be learned and grown in our lives.

Additionally, for the last decade, I have had the privilege of working with hundreds of leaders each year as a coach and consultant across the United States. In my work with influencers and leaders through the years, I have observed that teachability is hands down the greatest enhancer or greatest limiter to a person's success. I have long said, "Give me someone who is teachable and we can change the world, but give me someone who already knows it all and we're done for."

When it comes to learning about teachability, there are many modern-day examples we can examine, and we will, but some of the most powerful examples can be found by going farther back in history. In order to illustrate different insights about teachability throughout this book, we are going to look at a few case studies of historical figures whose stories are contained in a book called the Bible.[5] In addition to being a religious resource, the Bible contains many valuable case studies in leadership. In fact, some of the greatest and most timeless leadership lessons the world has ever known show up in its pages, and I consider it an invaluable resource.

But before we go any further, I'd like to offer this disclaimer.

If someone has put a bad taste in your mouth in the past by teaching the Bible in some objectionable way, I sincerely apologize. Unfortunately, some people in my line of work have been guilty of that. I hope this book will help reshape your impression of the Bible, at least in a small way. I would humbly ask, as you read this book, that you not tune me out or dismiss the points I'm making just because they have Bible references attached to them. I assure you, the data is factual, the events are historical, and the information can be extremely helpful.

If you are not comfortable with the Bible's being "God inspired," I completely understand that. For the purposes of this book, it's not necessary. I would simply ask you to embrace its historical viability as confirmed by both religious and nonreligious experts down through the ages.[6]

Finally, let me say that regardless of your religious background or beliefs, I hope to take an angle on these biblical examples that will not be offensive in any way. My purpose, as I have said, is to reference a few great examples of teachability—or in some cases, the lack of it. We all have much to learn on this subject, and I have found these examples are great studies. Thanks for trusting me to teach this subject without bias and with integrity.

I Want You to Reach Your Full Potential

Though I don't know you personally, I am betting that you're the kind of person who wants to be as successful as you possibly can be in the areas of your life that matter most to you. I know you dream of a better marriage, raising great kids, and leveraging your full potential in your workplace. I wrote this book for you. You're the one who is looking for that key to everything that can take your life to the next level.

I believe you can do it. Yes, it will take hard work, talent, energy, focus, time, determination, and so much more. But before any of those other things, it will take teachability.

Ironic, isn't it? A book on teachability that starts out by asking you to be teachable. I'm not guaranteeing this book will be an easy read. In fact, I'm hoping there will be a few places where you see yourself in a new light and it messes you up.

I hope you will get gut-level honest with yourself through the pages of this book. That might mean facing pain or insecurity you haven't been willing to face before. Or it may mean forcing yourself to apply the insights to yourself and not to somebody else in your family or your workplace. If you'll do that, I believe this book will change your life.

WHERE WE'RE GOING IN THIS BOOK

The layout of this book is strategic. It is broken down into three parts that contain five small- to medium-sized chapters each. And the book is written is such a way that it actually speeds up and moves faster the farther in you read. My hope is that you won't read this book in just one or two sittings. I hope you will take three weeks to read this book, a chapter a day for five days.[7] I want you to think of reading this book as like meeting a good friend for coffee every day and discussing a little more about the topic every time. Or maybe you'd prefer to think of it as letting me join you on the treadmill every morning for the next few weeks. You walk, I'll talk. But, honestly, I hope I won't be the one doing all the talking. I hope you will spar with the concepts in this book. I hope you'll let them mess with you. I hope you'll take notes at certain places, write stuff down, underline things, e-mail thoughts to yourself, talk to others about the ideas you find, and let yourself be changed.

I'm excited to see what happens in you as you dig into the contents of this book. I am confident your journey will be better and your life more complete because of it. Success in life hinges on one thing: teachability.

Now, go get some coffee and let's hang out.[8]

Matt Keller
@MatthewKeller

NOTES

1. In order to insert more content both serious and comical throughout the book but not break up the flow, I have put notes at the end of each chapter. I hope they're helpful and funny. But mostly funny.

2. Wait, you didn't get a manual for how to raise kids either?

3. Anybody else think it's ironically funny that I had to teach my computer the word *teachability?*

4. And by the way, if you're actually arguing with me out loud and you're in a public place like a bookstore or coffee shop, you might want to keep your comments between you and me at this point.

5. It's actually a collection of smaller books and divided into two main parts—the Old Testament, or story of the Jewish people, and the New Testament, the story of Jesus and the beginnings of the Christian church. And you can find it in a number of modern language translations, so it's not really hard to read.

6. If you're interested in some cool data about the Bible, here ya go. Josh McDowell and Dave Sterrett, *Is the Bible True . . . Really?* (Illinois: Moody Publishers, 2010).

7. Of course I'm giving you the weekends off! Or maybe you'll need the weekends to catch up if you're a slow reader. Either way, you get the point.

8. I consider us friends now, by the way. But sorry—you're gonna have to buy your own coffee.

What Is Teachability?

O kay Matt, if teachability is really the key to everything, then what is it?

Well, I could tell you that teachability means being teachable—which is true. But my mom, who was an elementary school teacher my whole life, would say I'm not allowed to define the word with the word. So that won't work.

I could break the word in two: *teach* and *ability*. But that's misleading. Someone's ability to teach is not exactly the point either.

I could actually do the dictionary thing and report that *teachability* means being "apt and willing to learn." But that still doesn't really tell you much about what makes a person teachable or, more important, how each of us can become *more* teachable.

So what I want to do instead is give you two words that capture what true teachability is all about and how it works in our lives. And when these two words are combined, they create a formula for teachability that has the power to change your thinking forever.

The two words are *desire* and *willingness*.

DESIRE

When it comes to teachability, the old adage is true: "You can lead a horse to water, but you can't make him drink." Everything we will discuss in the pages of this book will begin and end with desire. Without desire, our teachability is frozen in place. And when I say desire, I'm thinking of three desires specifically.

The first desire that is paramount to teachability is *a desire to become better*. Some people don't believe they deserve better. Some people can't see how their lives could be different or better. And some people believe they couldn't become better even if they tried. But teachable people want their lives to be more than they are today. They want to become better parents, better bosses, or better spouses. They are able to envision their lives being better or greater than they are today. That belief becomes the fuel behind their teachability, which helps them reach their full potential in life.

I have a friend who has so much going for him.[1] He's a college graduate who finished in the upper end of his class. He is really talented and could basically do whatever he wanted to do. If anyone has the ability to be something great, it's this guy. However, he has worked at the entry level of a multinational company for nearly a decade now and is stuck.

Recently, I had a conversation with him that crushed me. During our conversation, he began talking about how much he hated his job. He went on and on about how he didn't like the culture his boss had created. And to make things worse, one of his closest friends had moved away, so he was there all by himself.

Always eager to help someone make progress in his or her life, I asked my friend, "If you could do anything with your life, what would you want to do?" He sat there for a long time and then said four words that broke my heart. He said,

"*I*

    have

        no

            idea."

In that moment my heart sank, because I knew my friend was in real trouble. I felt like I was watching him die a little bit right in front of me.

You see, his issue isn't just with not having a vision for his life, though that is certainly part of it. His real problem is with desiring something better for himself. Somewhere along the way, my friend lost his desire to see his life become different from what it is. One of the defining drivers of teachability is a desire to become more.

COMFORTABLE AND FAMILIAR WON'T LEAD YOU TO YOUR DREAMS.

A second desire that is needed in teachability is *a desire to change*. Some people are stuck in their ways, and no matter how much you try and convince them, they just don't want to change. They like being stuck where they are. Apparently it's comfortable and familiar.

But comfortable and familiar won't lead you to your dreams.

A third desire that is needed in teachability is *a desire to learn*. Some people seem to be naturally endowed with a hunger to acquire more knowledge, understanding, and skills, while others don't come by it so easily. But even if the desire to learn doesn't come naturally, that doesn't mean someone can't develop it.

Over the years, there have been many things in my leadership journey that haven't come naturally to me—things like accounting, bookkeeping, or financial reporting practices, for example. However, because I had a desire for our organization to be set up and managed in a trustworthy way, I had to learn them. Looking back, I can see that learning those things, though undesirable to me at first, eventually became fulfilling.

That's the secret behind desire. Like a lot of things, the more you feed it, the more it will grow. Now, I'm never going to love accounting, but the more I understood it, the more desire I developed to get it right and be excellent at it so our organization could be better.

See how the three desires work together? When I had a desire to be better, then my desire to change and my desire to learn grew. Desire is paramount in defining teachability.

WILLINGNESS

The second critical component of teachability is willingness. You can desire something all day long, but unless there is a willingness within you to do something about it, you'll never change or get better.

I may have a desire to have sculpted abs and huge biceps and triceps, but if I'm not willing to get out of bed every morning, hire a trainer, and put in hours and hours of hard work over several months at the gym, it will never happen.[2] Desire alone won't get you where you want to go. You must also have the willingness to do what is necessary to make the desire a reality.

When it comes to teachability, there are two types of willingness that matter most. The first is *a willingness to learn something new.* This is absolutely essential if we want to progress at anything in life.

My mother-in-law recently told me of a friend who was deathly afraid of getting a smartphone. She had never had anything but a simple flip phone, and the very thought of having to learn how to text and download apps scared her to death. When my mother-in-law tried to explain the advantages of a smartphone, her friend got all nervous and fidgety and said, "No please, I just don't want to have to learn all that." This grandma is missing out on opportunities to connect with her grandkids as well as a sea of other benefits, all because she is unwilling to learn something new.

A second type of willingness that teachability requires is *a willingness to relearn what you think you already know.* This is a big one for me. In fact, for a long time, it was the primary definition of teachability that I would use when I taught on the subject: "Teachability is the willingness to relearn what you think you already know." That definition, though incomplete, has served me well right up until I wrote this book and needed to expand on it.

People who have a lot of life or work experience bring a preconceived approach and way of thinking to whatever it is they are working on. This can be a positive and a negative. It's good because their experience can save a lot of trial and error and help avoid missteps. But it's bad because that very experience can also make them close their minds to new approaches and new ways of thinking.

We all tend to bring preconceived ways of thinking into whatever present scenarios we find ourselves in—work, parenting, marriage, or even a hobby. In a way, it's inevitable. But teachability requires a willingness to set those aside and be open to relearning what we think we already know.

Dunkin' Donuts is a phenomenal case study for this kind of willingness to relearn. Over the last ten to fifteen years, the entire coffee-and-doughnut industry has changed immensely. When I was growing up, Dunkin' Donuts commercials consisted of a portly man with a creepy mustache who was awake in the middle of the night saying, "Time to make the doughnuts." And any reference to a coffee shop either brought to mind a dirty Waffle House or a place where hippies hung out in the sixties and did things that weren't legal.

Today, thanks to Starbucks, the idea of hanging out at a coffee shop has completely changed. And thanks to the Atkins Diet craze of a few years ago, carbs in general have become evil, thus making doughnuts very unpopular to a more caffeinated and health-conscious consumer.

Rather than fight this trend, Dunkin' Donuts moved their marketing and branding away from doughnuts and more toward coffee and healthy options. They could have stood up and declared, "This is who we are. This is what we know. And we're not changing." Instead they were willing to relearn what they already knew. As a result they have remained a mainstay of pop culture and continued to grow their bottom line.

For most people, the key to reaching a new level of success in any area of life has as much to do with unlearning and relearning as it does with learning something new. We humans are naturally more open to learning new things because they feel fresh and are fun. But the idea of relearning something we think we already know can be deeply threatening. It feels redundant, like added work. It can threaten our ego, and it can cause us to think, *I already know that*—or at least, *I thought I already knew that*. Or the more guilt-driven version: *I'm supposed to know that*. Or the worst version of all: *How do I not know that already?*

When we feel that way, our teachability shuts down.

Let me say it as plainly as I know how: there's nothing wrong with relearning something we thought we already knew. That's part of getting better. Willingness matters a lot in teachability.

DESIRE AND WILLINGNESS TOGETHER DEFINE OUR LEVEL OF TEACHABILITY

Here's where the two come together. Our desire and our willingness together form the basis of our teachability.

Roger Seip, author of the book *Train Your Brain for Success*,[3] presents this as a simple formula for calculating your level of teachability—your "teachability index"—in any area of your life. He basically states it as an equation, which I've illustrated here:

Desire to learn times willingness to change equals our level of teachability.

```
DESIRE to learn
X
WILLINGNESS to change
=
level of TEACHABILITY
```

Don't skip over that too fast—it's huge. Read it again. In fact, I recommend that you pull out your phone and take a picture of that box.

Desire to learn times willingness to change equals our level of teachability.

Now, let me take it a step further. Seip states that if you assign a number to your level of desire and willingness in any given area, those two numbers multiplied together determine your teachability index. On a scale of 1 to 10, the highest possible "score" would be 100.

Let me give you a couple of examples. Say that your desire to be a better parent is a 9 but your willingness to change is a 2. Then your level of teachability when it comes to parenting is 18. And with a score of 18, you're probably going to struggle in how you relate to your child.

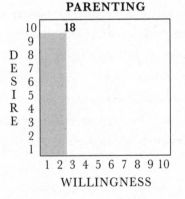

If one of your employees' desire to learn is mediocre, say a 5, and his or her willingness to change is a 4, then it is not difficult to see why his or her chances of success in your department are not looking good.

EMPLOYEE

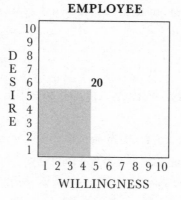

Or let me give you a personal illustration. If my desire to improve as a public speaker is an 8 and my willingness to change is a 6, then my teachability number in the arena of public speaking is a 48. Not bad. However, if I go through a lull and my desire goes down to a 4, then my teachability number drops to a 24. Not good.

PUBLIC SPEAKING

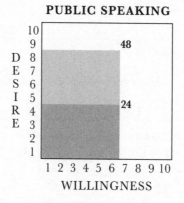

This equation gives us an instant lens to determine our level of teachability in any area of life at any given time. This is a huge piece of the puzzle for anyone interested in improving his or her life, because at the end of the day our success will come down to these two things: 1) our desire to learn and 2) our willingness to change.[4]

SO WHAT ABOUT YOU?

When it comes to your life in general, what number describes your level of teachability? When you multiply your desire to learn and your willingness to change, do you like the number you see?

Here is the reality. If your teachability number is consistently high in your life, then the probability of your reaching your full potential is great. If your teachability number is consistently low, then you are probably going to struggle throughout your life with moving forward. In either case, you're in control of your number—and you can increase it. Developing teachability is within your reach. But first we need to identify what might keep you from it. That is what part 1 is all about.

NOTES

1. *Not* this person's real name. I may—or may not—have even changed the person's gender.
2. How about we leave my workout habits out of this from now on?
3. I highly recommend this book. It's full of great tips and exercises for improving your memory and your mental capacity. Roger Seip, *Train Your Brain for Success: Read Smarter, Remember More, and Break Your Own Records* (Hoboken, NJ: John Wiley & Sons, 2012).
4. Did you take a picture of the equation? What if you make that the lock screen image on your phone for the entire time you're reading this book to help you get it into your memory?

Part 1

The Roadblocks to Teachability

If you run into a wall, don't turn around and give up.
Figure out how to climb it, go through it, or work around it.

—MICHAEL JORDAN

S everal years ago I was asked to do a one-day leadership training event in Birmingham, Alabama. Always up for a good
road trip, I opted to drive instead of fly. A friend who lives in
Jacksonville agreed to meet me in north Florida and keep me
company for a couple of days. Our drive would take us up
through the rest of Florida, north through Georgia, then west
across Alabama to Birmingham.

Unfortunately, what should have taken my buddy and me
eleven hours ended up taking considerably longer.

What I failed to notice before leaving my house in Fort
Myers was that Alabama and Georgia were getting a little rain.
And when I say "a little rain," what I mean is torrential down-
pours of biblical proportions. When we finally reached Atlanta
after driving nine hours already, we began to see signs declaring
that the interstate we had planned to take was closed because of
flooding. At first we didn't think much of those signs, but then
we quickly realized they were serious. When we saw the Army
National Guard standing in front of giant roadblocks with guns,
forcing us to exit, we knew we were in trouble.

Long story short, because of the roadblocks on the interstate,
we were forced to take two-lane roads all the way down through
the middle of the state in order to get back up to Birmingham.
That two-hour segment of the trip ended up taking five hours.

Roadblocks will do that.

They will add hours to trips that should take minutes. They
will add days to trips that should take hours. They will add difficulty to endeavors that should go smoothly. And while the
roadblocks my friend and I faced in flooded Alabama were there
to save our lives, that's not true of the roadblocks that can get in
the way of our teachability.

In part 1, we are going to identify five roadblocks that, when present in your life, can lower your teachability indexes and add unnecessary trouble and difficulty to your journeys. Learning to recognize them is an important first step toward increasing your teachability and reaching your full potential.

A CASE STUDY IN A LACK OF TEACHABILITY

As I mentioned before, history gives us many fantastic case studies on both sides of the teachability conversation. In the next five chapters, we are going to look at a man named Saul. He lived around 1050 BC and had the dubious distinction of being the first king over the nation of Israel.

Now, here's the thing about King Saul. If ever there was someone who was poised to be a pillar of the history books, it should have been him. He had all the attributes people would willingly follow. He was a man's man. If there had been Ultimate Fighting Championships back then, he would have been the champion because he was a crazy good fighter. In addition he was tall, dark, and handsome—definitely a lady's man. He was smart, charismatic, and highly skilled in a number of endeavors. Definitely king material.

From the outside looking in, Saul had everything necessary to go down in history as one of the world's great leaders. Unfortunately, that wasn't the case. His internal character didn't match his external abilities, and he lacked the one thing that mattered most.

Yep, you guessed it. Saul lacked teachability. And if anyone in history needed to be teachable, it was Saul. After all, he was not just any king. He was the *first* king over Israel, so he had a lot to learn. There's nothing like going first that creates the need to be teachable. If only Saul had understood that.

ALL THE RIGHT STUFF MINUS TEACHABILITY = THE LOSS OF TREMENDOUS POTENTIAL.

It's a pity, because Saul had all the right stuff. But as we will see in the next five chapters, all the right stuff minus teachability equals the loss of tremendous potential. It equals frustration for those around us. It equals pain and heartache. It equals confusion and a lack of trust. It equals the unfortunate legacy of being nothing more than a bad example for us to learn from.

That is the life of King Saul. His story is told in a book called 1 Samuel in the Old Testament portion of the Bible. Over the next five chapters, we are going to look at several instances where Saul's potential for greatness was stopped by the same roadblocks that threaten our potential for greatness as well.

We can get where we want to go in life, but we just have to deal with the roadblocks in our way first.

Chapter 1

The Roadblock of Pride

*A proud man is always looking down on things and
people; and, of course, as long as you are looking
down, you cannot see something that is above you.*

—C.S. LEWIS

S everal years ago we were asked to work with an organization
that had plateaued in its growth and was looking to identify
why. A couple of our team members flew into their city for a few
days, met with the leaders and the members of their team, and
then prepared for our usual debriefing session before flying back
to Florida.

But the debriefing didn't go the way we planned. Every time
one of our team began to offer suggestions, the leader of this
organization would cut us off. "Yep. Got it," he'd say. "What
else? Keep moving." It was clear this leader didn't really want
to hear what we had to say, and he certainly didn't want to talk

about any of the issues our team had observed. He thought he knew best how to run his organization, and he wasn't open to hearing any possibilities from outsiders like us.

At one point this man's wife, who was present in the debriefing session, grew frustrated. "Why don't you stop cutting them off," she said, "and just listen to what they have to say?" He ignored her.

Sadly, a few years ago the organization closed its doors and went out of business. It didn't have to happen. We could have helped them. The pride of this leader was a roadblock that kept him from being teachable.

Pride will do that. Pride will keep us from teachability and will keep us from getting where we want to go. Pride is a major hindrance to everything good in your life because, as we are about to see, pride breeds presumption, and presumption kills teachability.

TERRIBLE ODDS

In this first part of the book, we are looking at a leader from history, King Saul, whose lack of teachability cost him greatly. In 1 Samuel 13, we find a particular instance when Saul let the roadblock of pride get in his way. Let me unpack the scenario for you.

Under Saul's leadership, the army of Israel found itself in a precarious situation. To put it mildly, the odds were not in their favor. Their archenemies, the Philistines, were preparing to attack them and do major damage to them. Their intention was to take the Israelites captive, or worse, destroy them. The biblical account says that Israel only had about three thousand troops and the Philistines had way more, some translations say as many as thirty thousand chariots!—and a whole heck of a lot of people on foot.[1]

As a leader, Saul was feeling pretty unsure of himself and his army. Can you blame him? Any of us would feel the same way when facing those odds. But how Saul reacted when he felt unsure was what got him in trouble.

A DIVINE SAFETY NET

In those days, because Israel was God's chosen people, God guided them through special spokespersons called prophets. Only the prophets or priests were allowed to approach God on behalf of the people.[2] So, before a king went out to fight a battle, he would seek out the prophet to ask God if what he was about to do was a good idea.

The prophet would make sacrifices and listen to what God said. And if the prophet said, "Yes, God is in this," then the king could go forward in confidence. But if the prophet said, "No, God isn't in this," then the king would call off the mission. At least that was the way it was supposed to work.

Needless to say, King Saul needed some guidance before he led his army into battle against that huge Philistine army. So there they stood, ready to go into battle. Samuel, the prophet, had promised to come and ask God what to do. But Samuel was nowhere to be found.

They waited one day. Nothing.

Two days. Nothing.

Three days. Still nothing. Not a word from the prophet. And Saul's men were getting restless. Most of them, in fact, were completely terrified, and many were running away. Each day Saul's army was growing smaller and smaller. And the prophet was nowhere to be found.

Saul must have felt like a complete idiot waiting there day after day while his army dwindled and the Philistines loomed. Why was he standing around waiting on a prophet anyway? He was the king, after all. Why couldn't he approach God on his own? So Saul decided to do just that. The Bible describes it this way:

> Saul remained at Gilgal, and all the troops with him were quaking with fear. He waited seven days, the time set by Samuel; but Samuel did not come to Gilgal, and Saul's men began to scatter. So he said, "Bring me the burnt offering and the fellowship offerings." And Saul offered up the burnt offering.[3]

Saul let the pressure to do something—anything—get to him. He couldn't stand having his men see him just standing there, waiting, and he really couldn't stand seeing his army waste away. So rather than do things the right way, Saul just went ahead and did what he wanted. He let his pride make him presumptuous. And as soon as he did, everything began to unravel.

The minute Saul was finished doing Samuel's job, sure

enough, Samuel showed up. He wasn't even really late—he had told Saul from the beginning that he would be away seven days. Needless to say, the prophet was ticked when he found out what Saul had done. For King Saul to do an end run around the system was completely unacceptable, and it would eventually have severe consequences:

> "You have done a foolish thing," Samuel said. "You have not kept the command the LORD your God gave you; if you had, he would have established your kingdom over Israel for all time. But now your kingdom will not endure; the LORD has sought out a man after his own heart and appointed him ruler of his people."[4]

Saul presumed that because of his title and position he could do what he wanted—a big mistake. But as Samuel pointed out, Saul's presumption had made him untrustworthy, and that in turn made him dangerous as a leader. His kingdom would eventually topple, and someone else would be raised up to lead his people.

It didn't happen right away. In fact, Saul and his son Jonathan went on to win quite a few battles against the Philistines. But in the end, Samuel was right. God did eventually raise up another king, and Saul lost his kingdom.

Presumption, caused by pride, is a serious roadblock to teachability in our life. A presumptuous attitude makes us dangerous because it brings with it four destructive thoughts. When these four thoughts get lodged in our minds, our teachability is about to come to a screeching halt.

Four Presumptuous Thoughts
Caused by Pride

Presumption #1: "The Rules Don't Apply to Me."

Have you ever waited patiently for a table at a restaurant, only to have some hotshot walk up, demanding not to wait? I always feel sorry for the host or hostess trying to deal with that guy. Every time I see someone like that I always mutter under my breath, "That guy thinks the rules don't apply to him."

Pride is what makes us think we are above the rules. It's what prompted Saul to presume that since the prophet was a no-show, he could do an end run around the system and make up his own rules. Whenever we fall into thinking that we don't have to play by the same rules as everybody else, we have a pride issue that will get in the way of our teachability.

And here's the thing. This "above the rules" attitude is often easy to recognize in someone else (like the guy in the restaurant lobby), but often tough to see in ourselves.

What about you? Ever scoffed at the policies for expense accounts at work? Ever driven around the cones to park closer to a building? Ever sat in reserved seats that weren't reserved for you or tried to board a plane in a higher zone?[5]

Every one of us has moments in life when we're tempted to think we are above the rules. In those moments, we've got to have the courage to call our own foul. Assuming the rules don't apply to us is a subtle form of pride that, if left unchecked, can block our teachability and keep us from becoming all we were meant to be. Saul thought the rules didn't apply to him, and it cost him greatly.

Presumption #2: "My Position of Authority Entitles Me to Do Whatever I Want."

This thought roadblocks teachability because it puts listening to voices of authority in the "optional" category. When a child doesn't listen to an authority, we call it a tantrum. When a teenager doesn't listen to authority figures, we call it a phase. When an adult doesn't listen, we call it a problem. But when someone in leadership decides to make listening to authority optional . . . that's downright dangerous.

Saul assumed that because he was the king, he didn't have to honor anyone else's authority—not even that of Samuel, who spoke for God. He thought his position gave him the right to do whatever he wanted. His attitude was one of entitlement—another form of pride. He used his position of authority as an excuse to get his own way. And as Saul's example shows, an entitled leader is a compromised leader.

What about you? Have you ever assumed that your title or position entitled you to do what you wanted? Have you ever leveraged your position of authority for your personal ends?

Bosses, have you ever used "because I'm the boss" as an excuse to justify selfish or questionable behavior?

Parents, have you ever employed "I'm the parent, so you have to do what I say" just to make things easier on yourself?

Leaders, have you ever taken advantage of your position to get special perks or privileges?

It's a subtle and easy trap—especially for those whose positions do give them a measure of authority. Bosses have the right and responsibility to set and enforce policies. Parents have the right and responsibility to make and uphold rules in the home.

But the fact that we have influence doesn't mean we can take advantage of it or that we don't have to be under authority also. When we fall into that kind of thinking, chances are our teachability will suffer.

Presumption #3: "I Don't Need Anyone's Help or Advice."

When Saul felt the pressure from his army around him and got frustrated because things weren't going according to plan, his pride kicked in and caused him to think, *Fine. I don't need anybody else. I will just take care of this on my own.* His pride caused him to push something through prematurely instead of waiting on the right timing. And he ended up compromising the very thing he needed most—God's support for his rule over Israel.

When our church was just a couple of years old, we were meeting in a movie theater, and we had decided to add a second service in order to keep growing. We had been planning for months to make the jump to two services in September, around back-to-school time. And to spread the word about the new service, we printed up eight thousand dollars' worth of postcards. The plan was to mail them out to twenty-five thousand homes in the vicinity of the theater on the weekend before the new service began.

Unfortunately, that weekend fell right in the middle of the worst hurricane season southwest Florida had seen in forty years. We got three hurricanes in six weeks—all on the weekends, by the way. And the third hurricane was scheduled to make landfall on the Saturday night before we were supposed to launch our brand-new second service.

I will never forget my wife coming to me early in the week and suggesting that we postpone the mailing. I can still hear her saying,

"We wouldn't want those cards to be in mailboxes if and when the third hurricane hits. All that postage would just be wasted."

But I didn't listen. I wanted so badly to get that second service launched that I made the decision to go ahead and send out the postcards anyway.

Sure enough, the hurricane hit, and I watched as eight thousand dollars literally blew away. Most of them were never seen again. And the few people who actually did receive one weren't looking for a church, they were looking for their roof!

What a mistake on my part—ignoring my wife's very sound advice because I was determined to press ahead regardless of circumstances. That lesson in teachability cost me eight thousand dollars.

What about you? When was the last time you decided you didn't need to listen to anybody else? Do you consistently refuse to seek advice or blow off the advice you do get? Do you let your pride lead you to make unwise decisions?

Teachable people welcome input and feedback from those near them. They don't just push their agenda through while pridefully trying to figure things out on their own.

Presumption #4: "I'm Going to Go Ahead with the Good Instead of Waiting on the Best."

When Saul made the decision not to wait for Samuel, he settled for what he thought would be good enough—making the sacrifices himself and then moving ahead in his battle with the Philistines. But in the process, according to Samuel, he forfeited the best—having his kingship secured and established for the long haul by God.

Being teachable is serious business when it comes to our

influence. Saul's lack of teachability caused him to forfeit his trustworthiness, and that ultimately cost him his ability to lead. Saul had the right person around him in Samuel, but his pride kept him from being teachable enough to receive from him.

ON THE OPPOSITE SIDE OF PRIDE

A few years ago, Sarah and I became friends with Todd and Julie Mullins. From the moment we met them, we knew these were special people. They just have this air about them that is magnetic. And they're extremely successful as well—the pastors of Christ Fellowship Church in West Palm Beach, Florida, one of the largest churches in the United States. Their church has multiple locations up and down the east coast of Florida and an average attendance of more than twenty-five thousand people each weekend. Every week they are changing the lives of people not only in Florida but all over the world.

If anybody has a right to think they know best, it's Todd and Julie. If anyone has a right to be prideful, they do. And yet Todd and Julie are the exact opposite of proud. They are the most humble, teachable, and approachable people I know. Whenever we spend time with them, they always make us feel like we are the most important people in the world.

At conferences, Sarah and I are always blown away to see Todd and Julie sitting right up front, taking in every word the speakers are saying. They have every right to think, *What can any of these people teach us?* But instead they lean in. They take notes. They listen like crazy. They are two of the most teachable people I know, and they have the results to prove it.

Could Todd and Julie's success have to do with the fact that they *don't* have a prideful "I know best" attitude? I believe it does. Their teachability makes them stand out in the crowd.

WHAT ABOUT YOU?

John Maxwell wrote, "Pride deafens us to the advice and warnings of those around us."[6] That is exactly what happens when we allow these presumptuous thoughts to take root within us; we stop listening to those who could help us.

We must not let that happen. There's too much at stake.

As I said earlier, it's easy to see this stuff in others, but it's much more difficult to see it in ourselves. So take a minute at the end of this chapter and do a little self-examination. Review the four kinds of presumptuous thoughts that pride can lead to. Do any of them sound familiar?

If not, look harder. Better yet, ask a trusted friend or co-worker if you're showing signs of this kind of presumption—and listen to what he or she tells you.

If you have any reason to believe that prideful, presumptuous thinking is a problem for you, take a couple of minutes and e-mail yourself a note with two ways you're going to work on dealing with these thoughts when they arise.

You'll be glad you did. Pride is a teachability roadblock that you can't afford to have in your path.

NOTES

1. The Bible actually says they had "soldiers as numerous as the sand on the seashore" (1 Samuel 13:5). I told you it was a lot!

2. Thank God, it's not like that anymore. Jesus actually changed all that.
3. If you want to read this for yourself, the official Bible reference is 1 Samuel 13:7–9. I've quoted from the New International Version (NIV).
4. This one is 1 Samuel 13:13–14, also NIV.
5. What's the deal with all the zones that some airlines use anyway? Certainly somebody somewhere can think of a better way to get everybody onboard a plane, right? Call me, airline execs. I have ideas!
6. John Maxwell, "Pride—A Leader's Greatest Problem," *The Christian Post*, February 5, 2007, http://www.christianpost.com/news/pride-a-leader-s-greatest-problem-25618/.

Chapter 2

The Roadblock of Fear

*The first duty of man is to conquer fear; he
must get rid of it, he cannot act till then.*

—THOMAS CARLYLE

In 2011, the church I had led for nine years went through the most wholesale change we had ever experienced in our history.

For the first nine years of our existence, we had been a "portable church." That is, we didn't have our own permanent facility. Each weekend we would rent a high school, unload two giant trailers, and set up our entire church in two hours—lights, sound, kids' areas, foyer, coffee bar space, everything. Then, after our second service on Sunday, we would tear it all down and put it back in the trailers until the next week.

Finally, after nine years, we purchased and renovated an existing church, and in April 2011, we moved in. What happened next changed everything for our church and for me as well. Within nine months our church doubled from just under a thousand people to close to two thousand people in attendance each weekend. Seeing so many lives changed was amazing and a dream come true. But beneath the surface of that success, something was going on inside me.

Essentially overnight, everything I thought I knew about leading a church changed. And with that change came something I hadn't expected.

Fear.

Whether you're a leader of a growing organization, a stay-at-home mom with growing kids, a twentysomething about to get married, or a person in some other place in life, one thing is for sure: change is inevitable. To reach your full potential in life, you must be willing to embrace it. But change inevitably brings risk and its next-door neighbor, fear. And fear has the power to roadblock your teachability if you don't learn how to handle it.

The Other Guy in the David-and-Goliath Story

When I say the word *underdog*, who do you think of?

I'd bet that ninety-nine out of a hundred people would immediately think of David—as in David and Goliath.[1]

This classic underdog story took place more than thirty-five hundred years ago in a valley in the Middle East. And yet people in every nation on earth know the story of the little shepherd boy who beat a warrior giant with nothing but a slingshot, a handful of rocks, and a courageous heart.

What you may not know is that this epic battle took place at the same time that the Saul we've been talking about in this part of the book was king over ancient Israel. In fact, King Saul had a significant role to play in the story of David and Goliath.

Unfortunately, it wasn't a good role.

At that time in world history, war was a very hands-on kind of thing. Whenever a nation went to war, it was customary that the king himself would lead the troops into battle. He was considered not only the commander in chief but the chief warrior as well. In the case of Israel in that day, that chief warrior was Saul.

Now, when the army of Israel went out to fight the army of the Philistines in the battle that would make David and Goliath famous, the Philistines made a proposal. In order to save unnecessary bloodshed on both sides, they suggested, each side would send out its best warrior in a winner-take-all grudge match to decide the fate of the two nations.

The Philistine's choice was a nine-foot-six giant named Goliath, who had trained his entire life for battle. And from the other side, Israel's side, came . . . well, nobody.

The person who went out to fight Goliath should have been the man everyone considered the warrior in chief—King Saul. But Saul didn't go because he was afraid. His fear kept not only him but his entire army paralyzed for forty days.

Yep, you read that right. For forty days, the two armies stood on either side of the valley of Elah ready to fight and advance, but unable to because of one man's fear.

Now, here's the really crazy part: God had promised to fight for His chosen people, Israel, when they went into battle. But Saul still wouldn't go. Even with God on his side, Saul let his fear paralyze him. He chose fear over advancement, and it cost him for the rest of his life.

Let me fast-forward the story to the part I'm sure you've heard in some form or another. The little shepherd boy named David showed up at the battle and decided to fight Goliath. Of course, David won with nothing more than a sling and five stones. Even better, his resolve not to let fear stop him inspired confidence in the entire army, and they won a great victory over the Philistines that day.

Because of his courage, David became an immediate hero and the envy of the entire nation. But as for Saul—well, he lost more than his chance to slay a giant that day. The day he let fear roadblock him from the battle that was rightly his was the first day he began to lose control of his kingdom. History was changed because one man couldn't get past the roadblock of fear in his life.[2]

WHAT'S YOUR FEAR?

What a lesson to us all these years later. Fear is a powerful force that can keep us from reaching our full potential if we don't learn how to push past it.

In his book *Die Empty*, business consultant Todd Henry writes,

> We tend to think of fear as terror or shock, but in this context it means that we are paralyzed with inaction because the perceived consequences of failure outweigh the perceived benefits of success. This means that we are unlikely to try new things [read, be teachable] . . . out of a concern that we will pay a high price for failure.[3]

The easiest, most predictable, and safest place for a ship to be is in the harbor. But that's not what ships are made for. They are made to move through the water on the open sea. Yes, open seas are uncertain. Open seas are risky. Open seas are where ships sink. Open seas are full of unknowns. But a ship that never goes to sea is a ship that isn't doing what it was created to do.

> **PLAYING IT SAFE IS NEVER SAFE WHERE YOUR DREAMS ARE CONCERNED.**

The same is true for your life and mine. If we let it, fear will keep us from being what we were meant to be.

Fear always exacts a high price from our lives, and fear can take many forms. In this chapter I want to identify five specific fears that can roadblock teachability in your life if you let them.

Fear Roadblock #1: The Fear of Rejection

The fear of rejection will keep you from trying out, going out, and asking her out. It will cause you to shrink back rather than risk. It will cause you to play it safe, but the problem is that safe things don't grow. When you choose to play it safe, everything will plateau in your life, and a plateau is *never* where a preferred future takes place.

Playing it safe is never safe where your dreams are concerned.

In 2011, when everything started to change in our organization, the fear of rejection hit me big time. Up to that point, I was pretty comfortable with how we did things. I knew how to calculate the risks we took, to mitigate being rejected or judged by others. But now I found myself at the helm of an organization that was moving fast through uncharted waters, and every decision I made felt magnified and scrutinized in a new way. I feared doing something that might cause people to reject me, and that fear paralyzed me for a season.

What about you? Is there an area of your life where you are attempting to play it safe because you fear rejection? A relationship? A job opportunity? A financial decision?

Remember, playing it safe is never safe where your dreams are concerned.

Fear Roadblock #2: The Fear of Losing Control

The fear of losing control—of your environment or of other people—will roadblock your teachability because it causes you to close yourself off and not trust those around you. Consequently, you won't grow, which means you won't rise to a new level and you can't reach your full potential.

In a business or organizational setting, the fear of losing control leads to micromanagement and a refusal to effectively delegate. Through the years I have seen so many organizations struggle because of someone who couldn't get past this fear. I have seen eighty-year-old founders who wouldn't hand over the reins to their successors out of fear of losing control. I have seen fiftysomething business owners who are ready to move toward retirement but can't because they fear that the thirtysomething protégé won't make decisions the way they do. And I have seen younger leaders and entrepreneurs who lost their marriages or ruined their relationship with their kids because they insisted on handling every detail of their companies personally and had no time or energy left for family.

But fear of losing control isn't just a problem in the leadership and business community. What about the mom who keeps treating her teenager like a small child because she's afraid of letting him or her grow up? What about the dad who hovers over his children like a helicopter out of fear that they might make a decision that causes them harm—or, worse, that they might make a mistake and make him look bad? (Fear of lost control can be closely related to fear of rejection.) What about a friend-ship or a dating relationship that dissolves because one or both people grows jealous or possessive—another form of control?

The fear of losing control is real, and even though we can tell ourselves it's not rational, it still creeps in and stops us in our tracks at the most inopportune times. I have dealt with this myself many times.

Since that crazy season in 2011, our church has expanded multiple times. Just three years after we opened our first campus, we purchased and built another campus about twenty minutes away from our first facility. The new campus looks and feels just like our first campus,[4] only it gives us the opportunity to serve an entirely new group of people outside the radius of our first location. Talk about a whole new level of feeling out of control. With more than one location, there are programs, systems, and details I never see that affect our brand and impact people's lives every week.

THE ONLY WAY TO MULTIPLY IS TO BE WILLING TO LOSE CONTROL.

But here's what I've learned: the only way to multiply is to be willing to lose control—or better, to share control with others. Business consultant and psychologist Henry Cloud puts it this way in his book *Boundaries for Leaders*: "Great leaders do the opposite of exercising control over others. Instead of taking all the control, they give it away."[5]

The truth is, you cannot grow until you are willing to trust those around you—your employees, team members, family, or kids. Embrace the loss of control instead of fearing it. That's the only way to reach your full potential and achieve success.

Fear Roadblock #3: The Fear of Criticism

The higher you go in life, the more you should expect criticism. After all, critics only criticize people who are doing something important. If you're not doing anything worth noticing, then don't worry; chances are nobody will criticize you. But if you are trying to raise great kids, prepare to be criticized. If you are trying to start a company, prepare to be criticized. If you are trying to get in shape, prepare to be criticized.

Criticism is an expected part of the game for anyone who wants to be better than he or she is today. When we fear being criticized, however, we stop trying to be better.

Fear of criticism also makes us push others away. But it is only as we pull others close that they can help us—and we them. When we isolate ourselves, we don't get better, our products don't get better, our marriages don't get better—nothing gets better.

Again, I know what this feels like.

When we moved into our facility in 2011, we immediately added a Saturday night service to the two Sunday morning services we had been doing in the high school. Within a few months we had added a second Saturday night service, bringing our total to four services each weekend.

As you can imagine, teaching four times each weekend soon began taking a toll on me—physically, mentally, and emotionally. I found myself completely exhausted for the first two days of every week, and that exhaustion was inhibiting my ability to lead our team effectively. When I factored in other teaching I was doing, I really began to feel the drain.

Therefore, in February 2012, we introduced video teaching to our church. Each weekend, in one of our Sunday services, instead of my speaking in person, a video screen would drop from the ceiling in the middle of our stage and we would play a recording of the Saturday night message. Not only was this a benefit for me personally because I was relieved of having to speak in that service, but it also represented a huge philosophical shift for our church. No longer did I have to be present in order for attendees to "have a Next Level Church experience with God."

The trouble is, not everyone liked the new direction in which we were moving. When we added a third Sunday service that used video teaching that next fall, the complaints flared up again. Some were put off by the use of technology. Others felt slighted by not having me there personally. For some, church did not feel like church unless there was a pastor personally standing on stage delivering the message.

Now, the leadership team and I had thought this through carefully. We were convinced that the only way for us to move into a future that would include multiple locations was to use video teaching to do it. So we could not allow the fear of criticism to keep us from moving in this direction. We had to stay the course and do what we knew was right for our organization and for me as the leader.

Today, we have more weekend services with video teaching than we have with me in person.[6] And some people still don't like it. But there are thousands of stories of people whose lives have been impacted because we chose to face down our fear of criticism and make the change we needed to make. Their stories make it all worthwhile.

Fear Roadblock #4: The Fear of Change and the Unknown

Leaving the familiar is always scary. The fear of change is a roadblock to teachability because it causes us to live for maintaining the status quo instead of living for growth. In order to grow, you simply have to be willing to change.

It is hard to believe that just sixty years ago, African Americans did not have equal rights. They could not vote. They were not permitted to sit in the same section of restaurants or buses as whites. They couldn't even use the same restrooms as white people. Such a system is unfathomable to me. And yet many people in America feared changing it. Some were downright terrified.

Change in this area did not come easy for our country. Women like Rosa Parks and men like Martin Luther King Jr. gave their lives in order to make change happen. Thankfully, we as a nation eventually chose to move past the fear of this change and embrace a new way of doing things—and we are better for it. Today, some of the greatest thinkers, influencers, and leaders of our time are people of color. We even know what it is to have an African American hold the highest office in the land, the presidency of the United States. I am grateful to say that my close social circle includes people from many different ethnicities and races.

Now, please understand. I am not saying *all* change is automatically for the better and must be embraced. And change for change's sake only creates more work for everybody. We must of course exercise wisdom and discernment when looking at something new and different. But that wisdom and discernment are not the same as knee-jerk fear of the unknown.

Clinging to the status quo out of fear will never lead to a better future. But when we push past our fear of change and embrace the new, amazing things can happen.

In what part of your life do you fear change? In what ways are you keeping a death grip on the past when you should be opening your hand to the present and the future? Any area where you are allowing the fear of change or the fear of the unknown to hold on to you is an area in which you cannot move forward. And that area of your life will eventually become your lid. So many people with great potential never reach it simply because they fear change or the unknown.

Fear Roadblock #5: The Fear of Greater Responsibility

Thinking back over those months in 2011 when our church was experiencing such rapid growth, I can see that the pressure of added responsibility really messed with me. Anyone who has ever led an organization through a season of tremendous growth understands what I mean. You feel the weight of added employees, added work, added media coverage, added expense, added demands, and added expectations, all of which can add up to added fear. In that season, I began to see how unhealthy leaders could get tripped up by distractions and temptations that never bothered them previously. Added responsibilities can create fear, which can cause them and us to run to unhealthy outlets.

> **WE WANT THE POWER AND THE PERKS OF PROGRESS, BUT WE DON'T WANT THE PRESSURE THAT COMES ALONG WITH IT.**

The fear of greater responsibility will always emerge when we begin to take ground in the direction of our dreams. Often we want the power and the perks of progress, but we don't want the pressure that comes along with it. Anytime we let the fear of responsibility get hold of us, however, we are stunting our growth in that area of life.

In order to keep growing in our teachability, we must understand and embrace the fact that advancement always brings a trade-off. It is impossible to go up without giving up something. Such sacrifice can be scary if we're not ready or aware of it.

It is natural to fear the added responsibility that comes with success. Consequently, we may run from it, hire it out, or refuse to take it rather than growing through the times that stretch us and take us higher in our lives.

So what can you do when the fear of greater responsibility hits you? I recommend a shift in attitude. Try to see the added responsibility as a blessing instead of a curse. You are being trusted with more, and that is a good thing. You are being found faithful, and that is a good thing. The temptation to fear promotion is always real, but it never leads to greater teachability.

Pushing Past the Roadblock of Fear

When it came to facing Goliath and advancing the Isrealite army, Saul allowed his fear to paralyze him.

David the underdog shepherd boy didn't.

Looking back on the season of fear I faced several years ago, I'm so thankful that I didn't allow my fear to roadblock my teachability. Instead, I pushed past it and came out on the other side a better leader, with a better organization and a stronger foundation for the future.

What about you? Where in your life are you allowing fear to keep you in the harbor instead of venturing out on the open sea? Which of the five fears we've explored is the one that predominantly trips you up? What small steps do you need to take to run at your fear instead of allowing it to hold you back?

Why not pull anchor and start sailing toward your potential right now? Moving toward what you were made for is far more important than living another day anchored in the harbor by your fear.

NOTES

1. The one out of a hundred is my mom, who would say she thought of me because I wrote a book called *God of the Underdogs* a few years ago. Thanks, Mom. (Sorry for the shameless plug.)

2. Can you imagine every pep talk for all time being about Saul and Goliath instead of David and Goliath? Just sounds weird, doesn't it? By the way, if you want to read the original story for yourself, you'll find it in 1 Samuel 17.

3. Todd Henry, *Die Empty: Unleash Your Best Work Every Day* (New York: Portfolio/Penguin, 2013), 174–75.

4. This works much like a franchise model for a restaurant or retail business—think Starbucks or Chick-fil-A.

5. Henry Cloud, *Boundaries for Leaders: Results, Relationships, and Being Ridiculously in Charge*, enhanced edition (New York: HarperBusiness, 2013), 128.

6. I never speak more than three times in one weekend. It's just better across the board. I am a better dad, husband, and leader when I don't tax my body like that.

Chapter 3

The Roadblock of Insecurity

There is no such thing as perfect security,
only varying levels of insecurity.

—SALMAN RUSHDIE

I f you understood where we were at the time, you'd understand why I was so insecure. I was a twenty-seven-year-old kid
leading a little start-up church with no money, no building, and
no clue what we were doing. And I had been invited to a small
gathering of pastors in Little Rock, Arkansas—a new church-
planting group that called themselves the ARC.[1]

What I didn't know at the time, but would soon find out, was
that the people I was about to meet were some of the best-and-
brightest, up-and-coming leaders in the church world. Several
would become household names over the next decade. At the
time, however, the meeting was just small enough and the organization was just young enough that they let me pull up a chair to

the table. Before I knew what had happened, they were accepting me like a little brother.

Over the next couple of years at similar gatherings, I had the privilege of building relationships and exchanging phone numbers with some of the most influential pastors in America. They accepted me. But to be honest, I had a much harder time *feeling* acceptable around them. Every time I had the chance to hang out with these great men, instead of feeling excited to be able to learn and glean from them, I found myself intimidated and insecure.

Each time we were together, several of them would say to me, "Matt, call me. Text me sometime. Let's connect."

I'd answer, "Sure." But inside I was thinking, *Yeah, right. Who am I to call you? You're awesome and I am a nobody!*

To make matters worse, the next time we were together they'd say, "Hey, why haven't you called me?"

The issue clearly wasn't with them but with me. Insecurity was roadblocking my teachability with a group of leaders I desperately needed to learn from. Sadly, I have to admit that these feelings continued inside me for more than five years.

Thankfully, one of the members of this group I was closest to was Randy Bezet, who pastors Bayside Community Church in Bradenton, Florida. Because Randy lives just ninety minutes up the road from me, we get together two or three times a year at a Cracker Barrel[2] just to eat pancakes, hang out, and catch up. During one of our regular breakfasts at "the Crack," I began to share with him how insecure I felt whenever I got around "the guys."

After letting me share for six or eight minutes, Randy finally cut me off and slapped me in the face without ever lifting a hand.

"Matt, let me tell you something," he said. "We all see you as the successful, talented, gifted leader that you are. The only person who doesn't see you that way is you." And then he made a statement I've never forgotten. "I don't know what it's going to take for you to start seeing yourself differently, but you need to figure it out, or else you're going to squander a really great opportunity in your life."[3]

Finally, someone's words had broken through the roadblock of insecurity that I had let hinder my progress for far too long. I had a bottomless opportunity at my fingertips—the opportunity to learn from and to build relationships with some of the country's greatest leaders in my area of endeavor. And I had been wasting that opportunity because of my own insecurity.

MAYBE YOU CAN RELATE

It's possible, as you read my story, that your mind races to a scenario where you've done something similar. Perhaps there's a veteran salesperson in your division, but every time you get around that person you get cotton mouth and clam up. Maybe there's an upperclassman who lives down the hall that you're too intimidated to talk to. Perhaps you experience these feelings of insecurity when you open a book written by an expert in your field. Maybe you feel like you're not good enough when you see the other moms dropping their kids off at the parents-day-out event at your church.

Insecurity is something everyone experiences from time to time. But the fact that we all experience it doesn't mean we have to be led by it.

Unfortunately, King Saul in the Bible didn't get that message. As a result he allowed his insecurity to drive him farther away from his destiny rather than toward it.

INSECURE FROM THE START

When you study the life and leadership journey of Saul in the book of 1 Samuel in the Bible, it's easy to see that insecurity was an issue for Saul from the very beginning. In fact, when he was chosen to be king in 1 Samuel 10, an interesting thing happened. Samuel the prophet and Saul had a small, private "anointing" ceremony in which Samuel poured oil on Saul's head and basically declared him king over the nation. Then Samuel gave Saul some specific instructions and told him to meet him at another place later that night for the public declaration that Saul was going to be king.

Now, I don't know about you, but if that happened to me, I would be running around telling everyone I possibly could what had just happened. I would be setting up a new Twitter account—something like @TheBigDogKingMatt. I'd be calling my parents, texting all my friends, and Facebooking everyone I knew in high school with, "What's up now, people? I'm the king, baby!!!"

But that's not what Saul did. Interestingly, he kept it quiet. He didn't even tell his relatives that he was picked to be king. And when the time rolled around for the official public ceremony, the Bible says that Saul didn't even show up.

> Samuel had all Israel come forward by tribes. . . . Then he brought forward the tribe of Benjamin, clan by clan, and Matri's clan was taken. Finally Saul son of Kish was taken. But

when they looked for him, he was not to be found. So they inquired further of the LORD, "Has the man come here yet?" And the LORD said, "Yes, he has hidden himself among the supplies."[4]

Can you believe that? Saul was so insecure about being chosen as king that he was afraid to come out from behind the storage shelves. His insecurity roadblocked his potential from the very beginning of his leadership journey. And sadly, he was never able to maneuver around that particular roadblock. His insecurities hampered him throughout his lifetime and eventually cost him his kingship.

FOUR KINDS OF INSECURITY

Insecurity is a potential roadblock in the life of every one of us who desires to reach our full potential as well. In particular, there are four feelings of insecurity that can block our teachability if we don't know how to recognize them and deal with them when they arise.

Insecurity Roadblock #1: "I Feel Inferior."

Why did Saul hide in the storage area instead of coming forth to be named king? I believe it was because he felt inferior or "less than." And why did he feel inferior? Most likely because he was comparing himself to others. Rather than standing confidently in who he was—or who Samuel and God said he was—Saul gave in to the feeling that someone else was more qualified to do the job he had been called to do.

This is what I felt for so long when I got around my friends in the ARC. I would look around at all those impressive people and feel like I was unworthy to be there with them. And this feeling held me back from being able to be teachable around them. Yes, I would eavesdrop on their conversations, but I wasn't maximizing the opportunity I had been given.

Anytime we compare ourselves with someone else, we miss out on what we can be learning now. That's because comparisons inevitably lead to pride (see chapter 1) or feelings of inferiority. Either can hold us back from moving forward, but I believe inferiority feelings are especially deadly.

One of the biggest problems with comparison is that we are often tempted to compare ourselves with those whose circumstances are completely different from ours. We compare our weakness with the other person's strength and naturally come up short. Or we compare our lives in one "season" with someone in a completely different season. Thus a mom with small kids will compare herself to the mom whose kids are teenagers and more self-sufficient. A rookie in her first leadership role will compare herself to the leader down the hall that has been at this leadership thing for two decades. It's apples and oranges. No wonder such comparisons tend to create feelings of inferiority.

Inferior feelings prompted by comparison will sabotage our teachability because they kill our motivation. When we give in to feeling like we are less than someone else, we destroy our confidence and shut down any learning that is available to us.

Insecurity Roadblock #2: "I Feel Like an Imposter."
A second feeling of insecurity that can roadblock our teachability is feeling like we're faking it. There's nothing worse, is there? From the very beginning of his role as king, Saul felt like

he was faking it. Even though he had the counsel and wisdom of Samuel next to him and the favor of God upon him, he still felt like an imposter.

But it's easy to do, isn't it? You walk into a party, and everybody looks like they have it all together and you feel like a fish out of water. Or you walk into a meeting and everybody is speaking in jargon, using code words that make you think you missed a training class. Or you walk into a church where everybody looks like they just stepped out of a Gap commercial, and you've been fighting with your kids the entire ride there.

So you do your best to fit in—make small talk, try to look happy and intelligent like the people around you. Even though you feel like an imposter, you do your best not to let on. But deep inside you know you're faking it, and you can't believe nobody can tell. Even when you succeed and everyone compliments you, you have the sneaking suspicion that you've got everyone fooled.

When that happens, you've moved from *feeling* like an imposter to actually being one.

The problem is that faking it requires a lot of sideways energy and emotion and doesn't produce many results. More important, it creates an invisible wall that teachability can't get through. Faking it keeps people from seeing the real you and consequently keeps them from being able to help or teach you. It also can keep you from believing in your own success or giftedness or from accepting other people's sincere praise. Feeling like an imposter and faking to cover up those feelings is a lonely and nonproductive way to live.

Insecurity Roadblock #3: "I Feel Incapable."

Feeling incapable is the insecurity that arises when we think we don't have what it takes to accomplish what we believe is expected of us. I believe that deep down, Saul didn't feel like he was capable of being a good king.[5] That feeling roadblocked his leadership for his entire life.

When we honestly don't believe we have the skills or talent to do what needs to be done, we tend to shut down. This is often seen when someone starts a challenging new job or takes on a new role at work. Bringing home a newborn from the hospital can cause us to feel this way, as can many other situations. These feelings are normal and should be anticipated whenever we venture out in a new or unknown direction. Having them is perfectly acceptable, but allowing them to control us is not.

Every time we go after something new in life, we're going to be tempted to feel this way. Insecurity is built in to new ventures—that's just one of the facts of life.[6] It's like the side of fries you get with your burger at a fast-food place. So it just makes sense to expect those feelings of insecurity and prepare for them. Stand strong knowing that although you may not have all the skills you will need, you can and will learn what is necessary. You know enough to be teachable, and that is enough.

Insecurity Roadblock #4: "I Feel Unworthy."

If feeling incapable speaks to a lack of confidence in one's competence, then feeling unworthy speaks to not feeling adequate as a person. I believe Saul hid behind the storage containers at the public ceremony because he felt that way. I felt the same way at those early ARC meetings—like I didn't even belong at the table with these guys. I saw them as somehow higher or bigger or better than me. I had to work through those feelings of inadequacy in order to maximize my teachability.

Overcoming Insecurity

Every person on planet Earth struggles with feelings of insecurity at times. The feeling of "I don't belong here" or "I don't deserve the good things that happen to me" is an epidemic among so many in our world today. It's a subtle and often unspoken belief that holds many people back from teachability and reaching their full potential.

So what do we do? How do we overcome insecurity and break through this roadblock of teachability? Let me suggest three strategies.

Overcoming Insecurity Strategy #1: Embrace the Fact That You Have Nothing to Prove and No One to Prove It To.

To this day, whenever I find myself in a situation where I am interacting with influential leaders who would normally intimidate me, I simply say under my breath, "I have nothing to prove and no one to prove it to." This is a phrase I adopted years ago when I realized I needed to overcome feelings of insecurity in my life. You have no idea how much it has helped me handle the feelings of insecurity I may feel at any given time.

I HAVE NOTHING TO PROVE AND NO ONE TO PROVE IT TO.

Overcoming Insecurity Strategy #2: Start Believing That You Belong Where You Are.

One of the biggest keys to overcoming insecurity is knowing how you are gifted and where your talents lie. Knowing who you are and who you aren't can be extremely empowering. The more in tune you become with your strengths, your skills, and your God-given worth, the more confident you can become and the less insecure you will feel.

I will talk more about this in chapter 14, but for now, let me ask you a question: Do you believe you belong where you are in life? Why or why not?

In light of where you've come from and where you are headed in the future, I believe that where you are at this moment is exactly where you need to be. If you've experienced success, be confident that you're not undeserving. You're not an imposter. You're perfectly suited to be where you are. If you're in a valley season, know that you're not meant to be there forever. You are meant for more. You'll rise again. You'll make a comeback. Your life won't always look this way.

Once you can learn to believe and accept that truth, everything will begin to change for you, and your insecurities will fade.

Overcoming Insecurity Strategy #3: Know You Are in Process.

One of the most empowering strategies for fighting off feelings of insecurity is to remind yourself that you are in process. In other words, you're not there yet, and that's okay. You don't have to be an expert in order to stand confidently on your own two feet in the place where you are.

Yes, you're an inexperienced parent, but your baby doesn't know that—and you're improving every day.

Yes, you're the new guy or girl in the IT department, but you're doing your job, and you're learning every chance you get.

Yes, you've never created a website or written a novel or spoken in public before, but that doesn't mean you can't do it.

THE KEY TO EVERYTHING

Yes, you messed up that last project, but there will be others, and you'll learn from this failure.

You're in progress, and you'll get there if you don't let feelings of insecurity trip you up.

Insecurity is a silent killer of teachability in your life. Don't let it trap you in the storeroom when it's time to step up to your destiny.

NOTES

1. ARC stands for the Association of Related Churches. The ARC is a collection of pastors and churches who are committed to starting other churches across the United States and around the world. To learn more, go to https://www.arcchurches.com.
2. Randy, it's definitely your turn to buy.
3. Whether Randy said it with that harsh of a "dad" tone, I don't remember. But that's how I heard it and, hey, it got through to me, so I'm grateful.
4. You can read this story in 1 Samuel 10:20–22.
5. When you read these accounts of Saul's life, the Bible doesn't openly discuss his internal, emotional state. I am presuming that this must have been what he was feeling.
6. I loved watching *The Facts of Life* television show as a kid. Do you remember the theme song—about taking the good, taking the bad, and so on? Come on, you know you want to sing it. Go ahead—break through that roadblock of insecurity. (If you don't know that song, Google it. You might even find a streaming rerun of the show.)

Chapter 4

The Roadblock of Pain

Learning is not child's play; we cannot learn without pain.

—ARISTOTLE

S ome mornings I just can't do it. It's just too hard. The weight is just too much. The stress is too great, and the amount of energy it will take is going to exact too great a price.

Am I talking about getting up, going to work, and leading my organization well? I wish. That sounds like a walk in the park compared to what I have to do.

Am I talking about loving my wife the way she deserves to be loved or parenting my kids well? Ha! That's nothing compared to this.

Am I talking about writing books that change people's lives or crafting talks that change people's paradigms? Nope. That's a piece of cake compared to this all-consuming, horrifyingly difficult thing I have to do every morning.

What am I talking about?

I'm talking about picking out a shirt to wear.

Now before you judge me, which I know you want to do, let me finish. Everyone who knows me knows that I'm a "shirt guy." And by that I mean I never met a shirt I didn't like.[1] Some mornings I literally stand in my closet staring at all my shirts and think, *There are too many choices. I can't do it. I'll never be able to pick just one.*

In these moments of what I'll call my "first-world spoiled-rotten crisis," I will literally say out loud, "Stop being ridiculous Matt. It's a shirt. Make a choice and move on, because *no one cares but you.*"

Which is tragically true.

Once the words have had time to get from my mouth to my ears and into my head, then and only then am I able to stop hesitating. Then and only then can I reach into my closet and make a choice.

No longer do I fear the what-ifs of my lunch appointment later and how the shirt will make me feel. No longer do I fear the leadership meeting I have scheduled for three o'clock and wonder if the shirt will make me more creative.

No, in that moment, the moment where I stop being ridiculous, I simply make a choice and move on.

And the exquisite pain of choosing a shirt is behind me . . . for now.[2]

A REAL PAINFUL SITUATION

In this chapter, I want to talk about pain. Of course, I'm being silly about the difficulties of picking out a shirt. But the not-so-silly reality is that we all have pain in our lives—pain both physical and emotional, current and past. When I look back over my life and leadership journey in the past, I can see so many times when I have been hurt. There have been times when I've been betrayed. Times when I've lost friends. Times when people I never thought could hurt me . . . did.

You have pain like that as well, of course. We all do. There is not one person on earth who hasn't gone through painful situations in his or her life—and any person who tries to convince you otherwise is just a better liar than you are.

> **REAL PAIN OFFERS ONLY TWO POSSIBLE RESPONSES: WE CAN DEAL WITH IT . . . OR WE CAN REFUSE TO DEAL WITH IT.**

In life, pain is inevitable. And real pain, unlike my silly-painful closet routine, with its seemingly infinite options, offers only two possible responses: we can deal with it . . . or we can refuse to deal with it.

But refusing to deal with our pain—running from it, hiding from it, pretending it's not there—is hardly the healthy choice. Unprocessed pain cuts short our joy, our relationships, our careers, and even potentially our lives. Anyone who has ever stalled out, burned out, or flaked out has done so because of some pain in their life that was ignored or denied. And pain that is not dealt with properly can also become a major roadblock to teachability in our lives.

THE PULL-AWAY RESPONSE

Why does pain threaten teachability? Because it causes us to pull away from people and circumstances we could otherwise learn from.

Think about it. When you slam your finger in a drawer trying to get a spoon, what is your natural reaction? You jerk your hand away from the drawer, right? You may pull that hand back close to your body or tuck it inside the other hand. You may stick your finger into your mouth or put it inside your pocket to protect it from being hurt again.

Other areas of life are no different. Whenever you experience pain of any sort, the knee-jerk response is always to pull away and protect yourself.

When your spouse says something that hurts your feelings, you pull away.

When a team member leaves you hung out to dry in a meeting, you pull away.

When someone makes a nasty comment on your Facebook page, you pull away.

When your dad told you that you would never amount to anything—you pulled away then, too, didn't you?

Here's why this matters so much to our teachability. When we pull away, we are no longer in a position to learn from that person or circumstance.

With every knee-jerk response to pain, we become a little less teachable.

A WALL OF PAIN

But we're talking about a reflex, an automatic response. There's probably no way to avoid it, and it can actually be helpful, alerting us that something has gone wrong.

The problems come when we *stay* pulled away instead of confronting the pain and learning from it. That's what really wreaks havoc with our teachability. Over time, in fact, it can skew our overall outlook on the world. Over time, we can stop trusting the best intentions in others. Over time, that skepticism can become cynicism or even paranoia.

Ever known someone who was just flat-out paranoid? I would be willing to bet that his or her suspicious and cynical worldview started out as pain that was never dealt with.

Unprocessed pain is like a wall that gets built around the heart.

> **WHEN WE PULL AWAY FROM SOMEONE, WE ARE NO LONGER IN A POSITION TO LEARN FROM THAT PERSON OR CIRCUMSTANCE.**

Over time it compounds and builds on itself. With each new painful experience we choose not to deal with, another brick is placed in the wall. We become a little more self-protective, more suspicious of the motives of others, less inclined to learn from what happened to us.

Again, it happens over time. For a while, the wall is only a layer or two high, so stepping over it is not too difficult. Eventually though, if we do not deal with the pain, the wall will get higher and higher until, rather than being a minor inconvenience to step over, it becomes a major barrier in life. The wall can go up so high that the light of reality is blocked, and we cannot see the outside world clearly.

OUR CASE STUDY

Our case study in this part, King Saul from ancient Israel, provides a phenomenal example of what I'm talking about. Saul paid a huge price for refusing to deal with his pain, and others paid a price as well.

It started when Saul became wishy-washy in his allegiance and obedience to God. As a result, God decided to lift His hand of favor off of him—a deeply painful circumstance for insecure Saul. When that happened, the first layer of bricks was laid around Saul's heart.

One layer of bricks.

Things got worse when God put that favor on a young hot-shot kid named David.

Two layers of bricks.

David's influence grew, and Saul's diminished. For Saul, that was really painful.

Another layer of bricks.

Then Saul's daughter, Michal, fell in love with David—another painful blow for Saul.

More bricks.

And when the nation began to respond to David's leadership, Saul's pain compounded.

Layer upon layer of bricks.

One hurt. One painful experience. One rejection. One per-ceived betrayal. One by one by one, small and seemingly incon-sequential events added bricks to Saul's wall of pain. Eventually Saul had so much pain that he hadn't dealt with, he couldn't see straight. His built-up pain eventually affected his judgment and even his ability to perceive reality.

It got so bad that Saul had eighty-five innocent priests and hundreds of their innocent family members killed in one day, simply because he thought *one* of his men didn't support him. And that wasn't even true.[3]

How Should You Deal with Your Pain?

The wall that unprocessed pain can build around our hearts is serious. There is so much at stake for every one of us. We might not end up as a mass murderer like Saul. But we will never reach our full potential if we are unable or unwilling to recognize the ways that pain is dictating our decisions, our actions, and our attitude.

So what do we do? How do we deal with our pain properly instead of pulling away, building walls, and compromising our teachability? Here are some strategies I learned from a very wise counselor that have helped me.[4]

Pain Strategy #1: Acknowledge Pain When You See It.

It is impossible to deal with something that you won't admit actually exists. So the first step in handling pain productively is to acknowledge it.

Now, this is rarely a problem when we're talking about physical pain. When we slam a finger in a drawer, we *know* that hurts.

But emotional pain is often different, especially for men. Many of us have been taught to ignore our pain, to "suck it up" to the point that we don't even feel the hurt when we experience it. But we still react to the pain, so I've found that the best way to become aware of pain is to notice your reaction.

Watch for moments where defensiveness, negativity, and a "pulling away" reaction pop up in your behavior. When this happens, don't ignore it. Don't justify it away. Own it. In fact, I recommend that you actually write down what you notice. When you see yourself pulling back in a meeting, write it down. When you put up a defensive wall with your spouse or a friend, stop and write it down.

I promise you, you're not reacting that way for no reason.

Pain Strategy #2: If You Can, Deal with the Pain Right Away.

This is a goal to strive for: to learn to respond to pain as soon as you are aware of it, consider what your best reaction should be, and learn from what happened. Do you need to confront someone? Forgive someone? Is this a situation you can avoid in the future or one you simply need the grace to endure? Have you contributed to the painful situation or are you merely on the receiving end of someone else's issues? Not allowing the pain that comes our way in our everyday lives to build up is paramount to living a life of teachability.

There is great value in learning to process pain quickly. There is even greater value in leaning in and letting it teach you. But again, this is a goal, not a quick fix. If you've spent years denying or ignoring your pain—as I did—you probably need to do some work on your past before you move forward to a teachable future.

Pain Strategy #3: Slow Down and Dig Down to the First Pain.

Let me make a statement that may surprise you. The reason you think you're angry, upset, or defensive in a given situation may not be the reason. The boss or friend or spouse who upset you may not be the real reason you are upset. They may be just the top brick on your wall.

The reason we get mad at the top brick is because that's the one that causes us to stub our toes when we try to step over it. In order to get rid of the top layer of bricks that created the pain, we may have to dig down and figure out why the first layer of bricks was laid.

In other words, we have to identify the "first pain" that laid the foundation for our wall of bricks to begin with. When we are able to knock that out, the entire wall of pain will usually start to fall down.

I think Toyota was the first company to popularize the concept of asking "five whys" to discover what's really going on in any situation. Here's what that means. The next time you feel yourself pull back in reaction to pain, keep asking why for as long as it takes to get to the real reason behind your reaction.

Let's say, for example, that your boss offends you. In that moment, rather than just stewing at your desk, kicking the trash can, or going home and taking your frustration out on your kids, start asking yourself some "why" questions.

Why did what he said offend you?

"Well, because he criticized me."

Okay, and why does that make you mad?

"Because I don't like being criticized."

Okay, why?

"Because I think I did a good job."

Okay, but if someone doesn't think you did a good job, why does that hurt you?

"Because I tried my best."

And why does it hurt so much when someone criticizes your best effort?

"Because if my best isn't good enough, then I must not be good enough."

And why do you believe that?

"Because my dad told me that when I was playing basketball as a kid."

And there it is.

Asking "why" long enough reveals the first brick of pain in a wall that you are still stepping over today.

I promise, if you'll start slowing down and asking why when you feel yourself pulling away in a situation, you'll eventually learn something about the sources of the pain that are road-blocking you from teachability and the life you want.

Pain Strategy #4: Retrain Your Brain.

When you discover the root of the pain that is affecting your decisions, you will almost always find a lie. You might not even consciously believe it anymore, but it is instrumental in triggering your pain response again and again. In the illustration above, the lie was, "If my best is not good enough, then *I* am not good enough."

Now, old habits of thinking, even those based on lies, can be incredibly powerful. In fact, there is evidence that they literally change our brains. It's like they create neural pathways in our brain—think of it as "wearing a groove" in the brain—that encourage us to repeat thoughts and actions even when we know better. In order for us to live and function by a new truth instead of an old lie, we need to form new "grooves"—literally retrain our brains to believe and react differently.[5]

Let me give you an illustration. Suppose you've been taking the same two-lane road to work for twenty years. Then one day, the highway department builds a new interstate freeway between your house and your work. Even though the new highway is better, you may find yourself taking the old road almost without thinking. It will still take some time to retrain yourself to take the new road instead of the old two-lane road.

The same is true with the habitual but false beliefs that shape our responses. We must retrain our minds to act according to new truths rather than old lies.

My counselor told me that it typically takes sixty days or so to wear new grooves in our brains and create a new "knee jerk" to what used to cause us pain. What has helped me do this in the past is to make a list of the lies I want to tear down and the truths I want to reinforce. Then several times per week, say while I'm walking on the treadmill, I will speak them out loud in order to regroove my brain.

I am amazed at how well this has worked for me. I have discovered that there are new and better highways in my mind to be traveled, but it's up to me to start taking them.

CONCLUDING THOUGHTS ON PAIN

Every pain comes with two choices: We can deal with it and learn. Or we can refuse to deal with the pain and make matters worse. What about you? What pain have you been ignoring, denying, or hiding from that you need to start dealing with? What pain have you been glossing over that isn't getting better? What pain have you been hoping would go away but hasn't?

You have two choices right now: you can keep ignoring the pain, or you can take steps to deal with it. One choice will add bricks to the wall, hemming you in and cutting you off from the future you desire. The other will lead you to a freeway of greater teachability and open up a world of opportunity for you to reach your full potential.

Which one you choose matters a lot. I want you to make the right choice. After all, your future success depends on it.

But right now, if you'll excuse me, I've got to go pick out a shirt.

NOTES

1. Size medium, in case you were wondering.

2. There have only been a couple of times where I've stood in my closet for more than thirty minutes. Okay, maybe it was more like forty-five, but that was just once. Or maybe twice. I can't remember. Certainly not more than once a week.

3. This story is found in 1 Samuel 22:6–23.

4. Yes, it took seeing a counselor for me to be able to get to the bottom of some of my own pain. Listen, counselors aren't just for crazy people; they're for imperfect people—so we all qualify. There is no shame in asking someone who is trained to know more about a subject than you do (that's called a teacher or coach, right?) to help us become better versions of ourselves. In fact, isn't that in itself the essence of teachability?

5. Please note that I am a pastor and leadership guy, not a brain scientist. What I've described here is a layman's understanding of how habits establish pathways in the brain. Here is a link to an article I found helpful in this regard—it might help you as well: http://robertringer.com/creating-new-habits-by-cutting-new-grooves/.

Chapter 5

The Roadblock of Pace

Slow down!

—YOUR MOM, WHEN YOU WERE A KID

I have a confession to make. The manuscript for the book you hold in your hands was due at a really bad time for me. I had what felt like fifty million other things that were due at the exact same time I was finishing this book. The content for our Advance One Day business leaders' event we were hosting a month later was due. The content for the pastors event we were hosting a month later was due, as well. We were launching a mini fund-raising campaign in our church, raising money to upgrade some environments that desperately needed it. We were heading into the biggest growth season of the year for our church, which requires extra time for me in terms of message preparation. My kids were both heading back to school. And, as if all that wasn't weighing heavy enough on me, my favorite sports team, the Tampa Bay Rays, were in fourth place at the time and running the risk of missing the playoffs.[1]

But even in light of all that, I was moving along okay with the book . . . until the wheels came off.

According to the schedule I had created for finishing this book, I needed to have all the content out of my head and onto paper by August 1. That way I could take the last six weeks to edit and polish it before turning it in on September 15. And I had done that. It was when I sat down the first week of August to begin the editing phase that everything seemingly blew up in my face.

As I began reading, I realized the entire setup of the book was wrong. And when I say wrong, I mean, "This is good content but about 35 percent doesn't even belong in this book."

I walked into where my wife was sitting and said, "Honey, I think I have to start over."

To which she answered, "What do you mean—start over? As in, 'Oh no, my husband is gonna go crazy for the next six weeks and that is not gonna be a good thing at all.' . . . Start over?"

> **I WAS TOO BUSY TO WRITE A CHAPTER ON BEING TOO BUSY.**

Yes, that kind of start over. . . .

For the next ten minutes, she and I talked about how, with all my other responsibilities, the need to rewrite would probably put me way over the top in terms of my schedule and workload.

Now, the good news is that by the next morning I knew exactly what needed to be done with the book. I needed to write about the roadblocks to teachability, the last of which is the one you are presently reading. And therein lies the irony: I was too busy to write a chapter on being busy. How in the world could I write about being too rushed to be teachable when I was, well, too rushed to be teachable?

For the next two weeks, this reality played tricks with my head and caused me to have a severe case of writer's block, right up until the night before I was scheduled to write this chapter. When I lay down in bed on that Tuesday night next to my wife, in a "Hail Mary"

> "EVERYTHING GOOD IN LIFE, INCLUDING TEACHABILITY, LIVES AND GROWS IN THE MARGINS. AND AN UNHEALTHY PACE ELIMINATES THE MARGINS IN OUR LIVES."

type of moment, I asked her, "Honey, what is the number-one reason that an unhealthy pace is a roadblock to teachability?"

After fifteen seconds she said, "Because everything good in life, including teachability, lives and grows in the margins. And an unhealthy pace eliminates the margins in our lives."

And that, my friends, is why you have to make sure you marry up. She nailed it. One of the greatest enemies to teachability is the speed with which we choose to live our lives. When we choose to live at an unhealthy pace, our teachability drops off considerably.

If it's true (and it is) that everything good in life lives and grows in the margins, then why do we have such a hard time creating the margins in our lives that we need for all those good things to grow?

My friend Brady Boyd wrote a book called *Addicted to Busy* in which he described this scenario perfectly: "Ultimately, every problem I see in every person I know is a problem of moving too fast for too long in too many aspects of life. Every problem."[2]

Don't miss that.

Moving too fast . . .
    for too long . . .
        in too many aspects of life . . .
            is an enemy to teachability in our lives.

THE ILLUSION OF SUSTAINABLE

When it comes to keeping an unhealthy pace, here's what we tell ourselves, and I know this because it's what I tell myself too. We trick ourselves on this issue by saying:

- "But I'm talented."
- "But I'm having fun."
- "But I am doing what I love."
- "But the things I'm doing are all good things."
- "But I'm young."
- "But these are my primary earning years."
- "But I have a lot of energy that I would be wasting on something else."
- "But at least I'm not doing something destructive like drinking or gambling."

And then we convince ourselves that we can keep up our current pace forever.

Now I hear you saying, "No, Matt, it's not forever. It's just for a season."

I know. I've said that too. But let's be honest. One season

somehow turns into another, doesn't it? What was going to be an exception to the rule has now become the rule.

When we live for an extended period of time at an unhealthy pace, our bodies begin to adapt and believe that this is our new normal. So when we go back down to a more reasonable pace, we feel guilty, antsy, unproductive, less successful, and driven to pick up the pace again. And that, of course, perpetuates the cycle.

Turns out, being busy is addictive.

DRIVING IN THE POURING RAIN

As you've picked up by now, I live in Florida, which is a fantastic place to live most of the year.[3] However, the summers are hot, and they also include what is known down here as the rainy season. I don't understand it all, but basically, because of the barometric blah-blah-blah and the temperature of the water in the Gulf of Mexico, something or other happens that makes it rain like cats and dogs every afternoon from June 1 to October 1.

Well, we Floridians get used to the rain. And because of minor matters like errands to run and jobs to go to, we have no choice but to drive in it.

One afternoon last summer, I was driving in a torrential downpour while trying to listen to a leadership podcast I had downloaded earlier that day. As I whooshed along with both hands white-knuckling the wheel, doing my best to focus on the podcast, an interesting realization hit me: *I can't do this.*

Multitasker that I am, I discovered that it is impossible to process a leadership message while driving in the pouring rain. My teachability went to zero because of the focus that steering my car through a deluge required from me.

The same thing is true in our lives. When the normal everyday pace of life feels like we're driving in the rain, there is no way we can be teachable and learn what we need to learn in order to grow and reach our full potential.

It's impossible. Our minds and bodies simply don't work that way.

SAUL, THE DISTRACTED, OBSESSED LEADER

You knew we would bring this back to Saul, right?

Throughout this part of the book we've been examining the life of King Saul from ancient Israel as a case study of a guy who lacked teachability in his life. And in the previous chapter, we saw that God lifted His hand of favor off Saul and placed it upon Saul's son-in-law, David. (That's right—the young David of David-and-Goliath fame.) We also saw that Saul kind of lost it after that. He let his pain skew his vision and did some pretty crazy things.

But what we haven't seen yet is that poor David was the primary target of Saul's craziness. In fact, Saul became a man consumed with a single mission: kill David! No matter what extreme measures getting rid of David would require, Saul made it his sole ambition and desire. In fact, the Bible records story after story of Saul's complete obsession with finding his son-in-law and destroying him.

Here's just a small example, from 1 Samuel 24:1–2:

After Saul returned from pursuing the Philistines, he was told, "David is in the Desert of En Gedi." So Saul took three thousand able young men from all Israel and set out to look for David and his men.

Did you catch that? Saul and his army had just returned from fighting their formidable enemy the Philistines, which should have warranted a much-deserved and much-needed rest. But did Saul rest? No way. He was a man on a mission—a mission to destroy his son-in-law. So he rallied his tired troops and set off in search of David. He risked the lives of thousands of men in the hopes of finding and killing David.

The next several verses of chapter 24 tell us that while on this urgent mission to find and destroy David, Saul ventured into a cave where David and his men were hiding out. Luckily for Saul, David was a man of integrity and decided not to do the king harm, even though his men were urging him to do otherwise.

Saul should have been focused on his real enemies instead of the threat he thought David was to him. But because Saul was consumed with his obsessive agenda, he couldn't stop and think all that through. His pace clouded his vision and made him vulnerable—and it nearly cost him his life.

Something's Gotta Give

Trying to sustain an unhealthy pace over an extended period of time is an enemy to your teachability because it erodes the margin of your life, and, as we said before, the margin is where the good stuff happens.

Without margin, creativity stops.

Without margin, fresh ideas don't emerge.

Without margin, conversations that produce breakthroughs don't happen.

Without margin, you don't have the ability to grasp anything new.

Without margin, teachability dies.

A few years ago, I flew to a city in the middle of the United States to consult with a young organization my team had been coaching for about eighteen months. The leaders were hungry, teachable, and ready to learn everything they could from our time together. After spending a couple of days meeting with their leadership team and seeing for myself all that they were doing, the time came for our final debriefing session before I headed to the airport to fly home.

A few minutes into unpacking my thoughts, however, I noticed the looks on their faces and the glances they kept giving to each other. The looks on their faces said, *This is overwhelming.* And the glances they gave each other said, *There's no way we can do all this and keep doing everything else we've got going on.*

I stopped the meeting and sat down. "You know I love you guys," I said, "and you clearly have a desire to learn and grow. But honestly, I think your biggest problem is that you're trying to do too much. The best thing you can do is cut about one-third of your goals for the next two quarters and just scale back to a more reasonable pace."

The minute I said that, I could see the relief settle over them. They immediately recognized that what I'd said was true.

Their pace was killing them.

ARE YOU DOING TOO MUCH?

Is it possible you're doing too much? Are you going too fast? Quoting again from my friend Brady's book, "Speed is the single greatest threat to a healthy life."[4] Let that sink in for a second before you (ironically) rush right past it.

> **SPEED IS THE SINGLE GREATEST THREAT TO A HEALTHY LIFE.**

And I would add that speed is the single greatest threat to your teachability. You will never get where you want to go if you're moving too fast and doing too much. You must slow down enough to be able to learn what you need to learn so you can become what you want to become.

Often in our hurry-up lifestyle, we mistake movement for forward progress. Having a lot of commotion in your life doesn't guarantee there's a lot of progress. If you don't believe me, just watch a toddler for three minutes. Constant movement, little forward progress.

Are you doing a lot of moving but not gaining traction toward your goals? That's yet another reason to consider the pace of your life. Have you left some margin where growth can happen?

Just because you *can* do something doesn't mean you *should* do it. Not every good thing is necessarily the best thing. Only those things that lead you into a better version of you are the best things for your life. If you do too many good things but neglect the best things, you'll never end up in the best place you want to be.

COMBATING BUSYNESS

To improve your teachability, you must learn to combat busyness and control your pace. How? I'm going to suggest three simple—though not necessarily easy—strategies.

Combating Busyness Strategy #1: Turn It Off.

Let me start with a question: When was the last time you sat for ten minutes in silence?

If the very thought of that freaks you out, then this strategy is one that you desperately need.

At least once a day you need to silence your world. No phone. No e-mail. No screens. I challenge you to turn it all off for at least ten minutes every day. No noise. No music. Nothing but yourself and the quiet.

Just sit. Let your mind wander. Let your thoughts drift. You'll be amazed at what you hear in the silence. Silence and contemplation are lost values in the noisy, hurry-up world we live in.

Got that? Unplug once a day for at least ten minutes.

Now, once you've built that into your day, start thinking about weekly.

Here's another question: When do you take a day off? If your answer is "When I need it" or "When I can," you're in trouble. You need to start taking a day off every week. And I don't mean staying home to catch up on e-mails or take care of home projects. Doing something that refreshes you, something that recharges your batteries and doesn't feel like work will do more for your productivity, your teachability, and your happiness than you can imagine.

One of the greatest traps we fall into is believing we're too busy to take a regular day off. What a mistake. You will miss your full potential every time when you ignore this valuable principle.

You probably saw the next step coming: carve out time to turn it all off on a quarterly basis. In our work with high capacity leaders, we always teach them that once a quarter they need to take a "personal inventory day"—an entire day when they get out of the office and do a self-assessment of their entire lives. (This is in addition to the regular weekly days off.) Rising above your life every three months will give you perspective on your pace that you can't see otherwise.[5]

Finally, in terms of turning it off, you've got to disconnect yearly. My wife and I are borderline fanatical about taking a once-a-year "Mommy and Daddy only" vacation. We look forward to that time together because it is the one time all year where it's just the two of us being a married couple. Not work colleagues. Not parenting partners. Not cohabitants. We are husband and wife, and it's awesome! And when we arrive at our secret, undisclosed location, we always lock our cell phones in the hotel safe for the entire week![6] I can't tell you what a difference this schedule of "turning it off" makes for us. We always come back with a new level of margin in our lives.

Combating Busyness Strategy #2: Cut Stuff.

Let's say your doctor called you in tomorrow and said, "You will die if you do everything that you have scheduled on your calendar for the next six months." And what if he or she then demanded that you cut one-fourth of the commitments from your calendar?

No excuses. No exceptions. You can't leave the doctor's office until a fourth of all of your meetings, events, and responsibilities are canceled.

What would you cut? It's like the lifeboat game for your calendar. Someone has to get thrown overboard, so who goes?

Now, here's the trick to a healthy pace. Save yourself the doctor visit and just play the lifeboat game with your calendar now. Get ruthless and cut out a quarter of your commitments. And if you can't bring yourself to do it, then hand your calendar to your spouse or a colleague and let him or her do it. In a worst-case scenario, give it to your mother-in-law and let her have at it. She may be the only one who will tell you the truth about your pace.

Any of those people would love to whittle down your calendar for you—because your busyness is killing them too. And somebody's got to do it. Your teachability and your success are at stake.

Combating Busyness Strategy #3: Stop Taking Yourself So Seriously.

I have one final question for you. On a scale of 1 to 10, how much fun are you having in your life right now? Keeping an unhealthy pace not only destroys your teachability, but it also destroys your joy. The busiest people you know are *not* having the most fun. They're struggling just to stay upright.

So in addition to slowing your pace a bit, what do you need to introduce—or reintroduce—into your life to start having more fun? What hobby do you enjoy that you can't turn into a job? What can you do consistently that fills your tank and helps you enjoy life more?

In my world, fun is not optional; it's essential. And here's the coolest part, the next time you are smack-dab in the middle of doing something you truly love, something both fun and fulfilling, notice your level of teachability.

I guarantee you it's sky high.

Concluding Thought

Life is too short and you have too much potential to squander it by living at an unhealthy pace. You can't finish the race if you burn up your engine.

So slow down. Enjoy the ride. Remember that you only get to do this once.

An unhealthy pace will roadblock your teachability, and a lack of teachability will keep you from living the life you want to live.

And like the title of the book says, teachability truly is the key to everything.

NOTES

1. If you love your team the way I love the Rays, you understand.
2. Brady Boyd, *Addicted to Busy: Recovery for the Rushed Soul* (Colorado Springs: David C. Cook, 2014), 44.
3. I mean, if you like sunshine, beaches, palm trees, and awesomeness, then yes, Florida is the place to be.
4. Brady Boyd's *Addicted to Busy* again—also page 44.
5. Wayne Cordeiro introduced a great self-assessment tool called the "twelve dials" in his book *Leading on Empty: Refilling Your Tank and Renewing Your Passion* (Bloomington, MN: Bethany House, 2009). I highly recommend both the book and the twelve-dials tool.
6. If you're a parent, you may be thinking, *But what about my babies at home? What if there's an emergency?* Of course, we give a number of where we'll be to whoever is taking care of the kids (usually their grandparents). We just don't want to be bothered with texts and Twitter and the phone stuff that feels like our normal life.

Part 2

The Characteristics of Teachability

It's what you learn after you know it all that counts.

—JOHN WOODEN

When was the last time you met someone you had a lot in common with? Maybe it was at a conference or maybe at the grocery store. Perhaps you were riding the subway or sitting next to someone on an airplane when you suddenly began to realize, "Holy cow! This person is a lot like me!"

As an extrovert, I love it when this happens. I'm always excited to meet new friends, and it doesn't take me long to warm up to someone once I know we have something in common.

When it comes to the subject of this book, teachability, it turns out there are a lot of commonalities in people who possess it. In fact, the most teachable people in the world all share similar traits. In this part of the book, we are going to look at five of these characteristics. We are going to explore several present-day examples as well as that of one particular historical figure who will serve as our next case study on what teachability looks like.

And here's something really interesting. The man we are going to point to repeatedly started out in life with the name of Saul—like the King Saul we have been talking about in the last five chapters. But this Saul is a completely different character that lived in a different time of history. And fortunately he is better known by another name: Paul. Also known as the apostle Paul, this remarkable man lived in the decades after Jesus had been on earth. His life and his leadership journey were pivotal in shaping the lives of millions of people not only then but now.

I believe Paul to be one of the most teachable people to have ever walked the earth, but he didn't start out that way. In fact, when he first showed up in the Bible, he was one of the most *un*teachable people around.

The book of Acts, in the New Testament portion of the Bible, tells the story of a movement that broke out in Jerusalem after the death and resurrection of Jesus. It was led by the followers of Jesus, also known as Christians. This movement quickly began to spread to other towns and villages across that entire region of the world.

But not everyone was excited about this turn of events. Many in the established religious community wanted nothing to do with this "good news" message that was sweeping the land. And one of the most outspoken voices against the Christians was this man named Saul, whose name would later be changed to Paul.[1]

Paul was one of the high achievers in Jerusalem's religious community. He had won every award possible, earned every bonus possible, and had become a big name among the old guard. He was extremely successful and consequently not very open to the new message coming from this seemingly rogue group.

Paul was so passionately against this new message, in fact, that he resorted to violence. History records that he was involved with putting Christians to death in order to get them to shut up. Talk about unteachable.

But then Paul had a face-to-face, knock-you-off-your-present-course encounter that changed everything in his life.[2] In this one moment, Paul was given a choice. He could surrender his prideful and arrogant attitude and lifestyle, embrace teachability, and have a chance to change the world; or he could refuse to become teachable, maintain his present course, and ultimately fade into irrelevance.

Thankfully, Paul chose teachability. Because of this choice, he moved from hating this new message to embracing it. In fact, he became one of its greatest advocates. Paul ended up traveling throughout the known world and is credited with taking the message of Christianity farther than any other person in history.

Some two thousand years later, the message of Christianity is alive and thriving across the four corners of the globe— and it can all be traced back to one man, the apostle Paul. Additionally, Paul wrote two-thirds of the New Testament. His writings have impacted the world in greater ways than perhaps any other human being ever. His writings are more widely read than Shakespeare, Tolstoy, Charles Dickens, and J. K. Rowling combined.

Paul's life and legacy continue to change lives today—all because he chose teachability. He is the perfect case study for an exploration of what true teachability looks like. My hope is that what happened to Paul will happen to you as you read. I want this book to be a knock-you-off-your-present-course moment for you as well. I hope the challenge to not only understand teachability, but also to embrace it as a lifelong pursuit, will capture your attention and your focus forever.

> **I WANT THIS BOOK TO BE A KNOCK-YOU-OFF-YOUR-PRESENT-COURSE MOMENT FOR YOU AS WELL.**

I believe there are countless lives that stand to be impacted by your decision to embrace teachability. Your life matters for more than just what you can see in the here and now. Like Paul's, your life is meant to impact so many others, and teachability is the key to that happening.

In the next five chapters, then, we will examine the five characteristics that the most teachable people in the world have in common. I hope that in some you'll see yourself perfectly as you are and in others you will see where you stand to improve.

Paul embodied all five characteristics, and he changed the

world. I am confident that when you embody them, you'll do the same.

NOTES

1. After Saul had his life-changing encounter, his name was changed from Saul to Paul. But in the coming chapters, to cut down on confusion, I will only refer to him as Paul.
2. The entire story of Paul's life-changing encounter can be found in chapter 9 of the book of Acts. It's definitely worth reading.

Chapter 6

An Insatiable Desire to Learn and Grow

The cure for boredom is intentional and applied curiosity.

—TODD HENRY

My wife's grandfather's name is Jim. He's in his late eighties, lives in Indiana, and is truly remarkable. A member of the so-called Greatest Generation, Jim was extremely successful in business and leadership. He raised five children over his lifetime and was also very active in every community in which he lived. At the time of this writing, he still plays tennis two times a week, takes care of his house and yard, and visits us in Florida at least once a year.

I always love Jim's visits. Not only does he have great stories to tell, but the guy is interested in everything. He's always curious, always wanting to learn more.

The last time he came to visit, my mother-in-law noticed him walking around the perimeter of our house.[1] She watched him for a minute, then saw him stop and lean over in front of the air-conditioning units on the side of our house. When she went out a few minutes later to check on him, he calmly replied, "I have never seen an air-conditioning unit quite like this, and I just had to stop and learn how it is different from my unit up north."

Two trips before that, Jim wanted us to teach him how to video chat on his smartphone, and the time before that, he asked my teenage son, Will, to teach him how to send a whole group of photos at the same time. Most people, as they grow older, become more stuck in their ways. Not Grandpa Jim. He's one of the most teachable people I know—mostly because he has an insatiable desire to learn.

DESIRE

In the introduction of the book, we talked about desire as one of the two biggest components in the definition of teachability. In this chapter I want to take that idea a step further.

When you study the life of Paul, who is our case study in this part of the book, it doesn't take long to see that he had an insatiable desire to learn. He never allowed himself to have an arrival mentality. He never thought he had learned so much that he couldn't improve himself in some way.

In Acts 17, we find an interesting pattern that emerges in Paul's life. Whenever he would enter a new city—in this case, Thessalonica—he would go straight to the synagogue, which was the center of learning in a city in those days. Verse 2 tells us what he did there. It says, "As was his custom, Paul went into the synagogue, and on three Sabbath days he reasoned with them from the Scriptures."

Was Paul there just to give his opinion and teach? I don't think so. Synagogues were the centers of learning and discussion for Jews in that day. The fact that Paul had a custom of going there indicated that he wasn't going just to teach but to listen and learn as well. Paul obviously had much to offer in the conversations that took place there among the city's most intelligent thought leaders, but he probably listened to the city's best thinkers as well and enjoyed discussing issues of all kinds with them. If he didn't, surely he wouldn't have been allowed back three weeks in a row.

I believe it was Paul's teachability, demonstrated by his habit of going to the synagogue to learn, that gave him the authority to speak and influence others with his message. If he had come in as an obnoxious know-it-all, his voice and message would have been minimized.

What an example for us as well. If we are ever going to reach the full measure of success we desire in our life, it will happen in direct correlation to developing a desire for learning.

IS DESIRE BORN OR DEVELOPED?

Have you ever seen those commercials for Maybelline cosmetics: "Maybe she's born with it. Maybe it's Maybelline"?

It's a great slogan. It also hints at a question that has been asked about many forms of human experience. It's the age-old question of nature vs. nurture. Are certain traits inborn or acquired? Do we arrive on earth as the persons we'll always be, or do we become ourselves as we grow?

It's a trick question, of course. In most circumstances, the answer to the question of nature or nurture is . . . yes. That is, we are born with certain characteristics that stay with us all our lives—personality, aptitudes, even interests. But we are also inevitably shaped and changed by our environment as we grow.

That's true of the desire to learn as well. It is true that some people are born with a stronger drive to find out about the world than others are. Some people are naturally more curious, more driven to acquire information. But that doesn't mean that every single one of us can't develop this desire in our life as well.

Here's the cool thing about us humans: whatever we feed, grows. So when we choose to feed our desire to learn and grow every day, that desire will grow in us. I promise you.

I love the story of Dustin Pedroia, the four-time All-Star second baseman for the Boston Red Sox. At just five feet seven inches tall and 170 pounds, he shouldn't even be in the Big Leagues, but he is. And he's far more than an average player. Dustin was voted the American League Rookie of the Year in 2007, won the American League MVP award in 2008, and has been a major contributor to two Red Sox World Series victories.

Growing up, Dustin had one person after another tell him that he didn't have the goods to play at the Major League level, but his overwhelming desire to learn and grow trumped the naysayers. The game of baseball is a very nuanced and detailed game. Men play their entire lives and never fully master it. Becoming a great player requires drive, determination, and a teachable spirit to the core. That's Dustin Pedroia. In his book, *Born to Play*,[2] Dustin talks about how from Little League on, he was always the youngest player on the team. He loved playing with kids older than him because it forced him to learn strategy and get better both mentally in his approach to the game and physically in his ability to play the game.

Dustin Pedroia has never lost that insatiable desire to learn and keep getting better. Even now, after becoming one of the Major League's top second basemen, Dustin still learns from his teammates and others across the league. Dustin spends time studying, watching, and learning from the best players in the game today. He's a model of teachability for us all.

Feeding Your Desire to Learn

Why shouldn't this be said of us in regard to our teachability and our desire to become insatiable learners? It can. The only thing holding you back is you. In the remainder of this chapter, I want to suggest six ways to feed your desire to learn.

Feeding Strategy #1: Start Expanding Your Inputs.
Teachable people crave input of all kinds and from every direction. When you're hungry to learn, new ideas and information can come from inside or outside your areas of passion and experience. Teachable people know that growth brings growth. In other words, when you are diligent to learn something in one area, what you've learned will affect your growth in other areas as well. When you push yourself to find input from all directions, you will expand the capacity of your mind to learn and retain that which matters most to the specific development of your career and life.

What are three areas of your life in which you could learn something new in the next seven days? Maybe it's a business principle or a social media skill. Maybe it's a hobby you've been interested in recently—or your spouse's hobby. Maybe you could download a new book about movie production or watch a cooking video on YouTube. Just start learning, then watch what happens.

Feeding Strategy #2: Improve the Abilities You Already Have.

I have been a baseball fan for as long as I can remember. I can still hear the play-by-play announcer on the radio as I sat with my grandfather in his room and listened to the Chicago Cubs game on his AM radio each day after school. And the first time my dad took me to Wrigley Field to watch the Cubs play—what a thrill. I can still feel the buzz of walking into that stadium, with thousands of fans rushing through the concourse around me. I remember the smell of popcorn, the taste of a hot dog wrapped in foil, and the crack of the bat echoing through the upper deck. I sat on my dad's lap most of the game, wearing my glove because I just knew the ball was coming to me. I remember feeling like I was a part of the game—and loving it.[3]

As I said earlier, baseball is a very complex and detailed game. It is those very details that make the game so interesting to me. For example, baseball is the only game where the defense controls the ball. When you think that some golfers can't hit a ball that is sitting still on a tee, but baseball players can hit a ball being hurled at them at ninety miles per hour—well, I find that simply amazing. Ted Williams, arguably the greatest hitter of all time, is famous for saying, "The hardest thing to do in baseball is to hit a round baseball with a round bat, squarely."

Having played the game as a kid myself, I couldn't agree more. But I have always been fascinated by how the best hitters in baseball, men who have been playing their entire lives, still love to talk about how to become better hitters. They study their own swing on video. They watch other hitters' techniques, enlist the help of a hitting coach, and seek out any opportunity to improve. Maybe that's why the best hitters in the game are the best hitters in the game!

Learning is not just a matter of acquiring new skills and information. Teachable people also want to improve in areas where they're already proficient. They don't rest on their laurels. Instead, they're always trying to improve.

What about you? Do you have that burning desire to sharpen the skills you already have and add to knowledge you've already acquired? What would your colleagues say if I asked them? What would your boss say? What would your spouse and friends say? No matter how good you are at something, there's always room for improvement . . . and growth.

Feeding Strategy #3: Prioritize Reaching Your Potential Over Everything Else.

We would all agree that change is necessary for growth. But the reality is that most human beings change only when staying the same is more painful than changing. Why is the victim of a heart attack now motivated to eat healthy and exercise every day? Because the symptoms and results of heart disease were more uncomfortable than developing new habits.

That's typical human nature—but it's not typical for teachable people. Truly teachable people don't wait for tragedy to strike before they embrace change. They understand that tapping into their untapped potential is better than existing as they presently are. This truth drives their desire to learn. Can the same be said of you? Is the priority of reaching your full potential more important to you than staying as you presently are?

Feeding Strategy #4: Cultivate Your Curiosity.

Curiosity comes naturally to us when we are children, but the older we get, the more we must choose to be curious about the world around us. As author Todd Henry writes in *Die Empty,* "In dealing with the pragmatic elements of daily life and work, our curiosity can become worn and obscured by a tangle of tasks and expectations."[4] In other words, life has a way of killing our curiosity—if we let it.

Why does curiosity matter? It's the energy that drives the desire to learn. Curiosity keeps our minds active and sharp, our thoughts young. It spurs us to look beyond the surface to find the truth, prompts us to ask questions instead of accepting the status quo. It's a doorway to adventure, drawing us to discover new possibilities we hadn't even thought of before. Curiosity is the constant friend to teachable people.

Now, I recognize the naysayer might ask whether curiosity is such a good thing. After all, didn't curiosity kill the cat? Maybe, but there's a couple of pieces of good news: (1) You're not a cat and, (2) There's a 74 percent chance you don't like cats much anyway.[5] But all joking aside, how curious are you in your daily life? Teachable people understand that it's important to constantly keep one eye open for something new to see and learn.

Feeding Strategy #5: Be Willing to Pay the Price to Learn.

For nearly twenty years now, the greatest and most consistent mentor in my life has been author and leadership expert John

Maxwell. His books, teachings, and personal perspectives have shaped me more than any other leader has in my lifetime. And one of the most powerful lessons I learned from John Maxwell concerned paying whatever price it took to learn.

Early in my own leadership journey, I read that John used to plan his family vacations around opportunities to spend an hour with a leader he admired. He would write to these leaders and offer to pay them a hundred dollars just to spend an hour with them. Now in those days, a hundred dollars was a lot of money—more like six hundred dollars today. But that was a sacrifice he chose to make, the price he chose to pay to learn.

A few years ago, when I began to pay serious attention to developing my writing career, I had the same urging inside of me. One of the authors I admired most at that time was Mark Batterson. (I still admire his writing today, by the way!) Mark was a pastor like me, and he was also one of the most widely read authors in his genre. I reached out to Mark through e-mail and told him I was planning to be in the DC area (where he lived) in the next few months. If he was available, I ventured, I would love to come and ask him some questions about writing.

Long story short, he agreed. So you know what I did next?

I planned a trip to DC!

Yes, that trip cost me plane tickets for my wife and me, a few nights in a hotel, and two tickets to a Washington Nationals game.[6] But it was worth every penny to spend ninety minutes with Mark Batterson. Today I am privileged to call Mark a friend and to have his endorsement on this book. You just never know what dividends an investment in learning will yield.

Becoming everything you were created to be will require making sacrifices and paying a price. Sometimes the price will be financial. Going to conferences, buying books, and investing in yourself is not cheap. But if you are not willing to invest in yourself, then you will never reach your full potential. Don't sell yourself short simply because it costs money.

Feeding Strategy #6: Be Willing to Delay Gratification for the Sake of Growth.

Teachable people not only understand that there is a price to be paid to reach their potential; they also understand that it takes time and commitment. When it comes to our development we can either pay now and play later or play now and pay later. Every day we decide. There may even be times when we have to go without in order to learn and grow.

In 2011, the Indianapolis Colts had a hard decision to make. Their veteran quarterback, the great Peyton Manning, had been the face of the franchise for more than a decade, but he had injured his neck and would be unable to play for an entire season. Although he was rehabbing and wanting to play again, there was no guarantee he would be able to do what he had done before.

The Colts had to decide to either take a chance on Peyton's uncertain health and hopefully win for a few more years with him or to release him and draft the number-one quarterback out of college, Andrew Luck. Doing so would mean that they would probably be mediocre for the next few years while Luck learned to play in the NFL.

On March 7, 2012, the Colts made their decision. They decided to part ways with Manning and be patient with the quarterback of the future, Andrew Luck. That decision cost them in the short run but paid off in the long run. As this book goes to press, Andrew Luck is one of the top-rated quarterbacks in the

NFL, and in the 2014 playoffs, Andrew Luck and the Colts actually beat Peyton Manning and the Denver Broncos!

What about you? Are you willing to give up some success and accolades now in order to keep learning and growing? Are you willing to forgo some of the limelight now so you can reach your full potential later? Are you willing to put in the necessary hours now to reap benefits in the future?

Todd Henry says it this way: "The seeds of tomorrow's brilliance are planted in the soil of today's activity."[7] The most teachable people in the world understand this and are willing to plant today so they can harvest tomorrow.

Concluding Thoughts

High teachability people have an insatiable desire to learn and are always asking, "How can I get better?" Their craving for input is without limit. Over the years, I have discovered that if I am not learning, then I am dying on the inside. Teachable people dry up fast when they're not learning, growing, and being stretched in some way.

What can you begin doing this week to feed your desire to learn, so you can reach your full potential? How you answer that question will determine your level of success in the future.

NOTES

1. My mother-in-law lives with us. It's an amazing arrangement. I'm so thankful for my mother-in-law, Alison.
2. Dustin Pedroia with Edward J. Delaney, *Born to Play: My Life in the Game* (New York: Simon Spotlight Entertainment, 2009).

THE KEY TO EVERYTHING

3. Every Chicago Cubs fan understands this "love the game" thing I'm talking about, because when you lose as much as the Cubs have for the last 110 years and counting, you either learn to love losing or learn to love the game of baseball itself. I chose the latter.

4. Another great quote from Todd Henry's *Die Empty*, this one from page 37.

5. According to a Fox News survey, 74 percent of people like dogs a lot, while only 41 percent of people like cats a lot. Enough said. See http://bit.ly/ioeoslafa.

6. One of my life goals is to watch a game in each of the thirty MLB stadiums. I was able to knock off another one that night in Washington, DC.

7. And here's Todd Henry again, also from page 37. Seriously, *Die Empty* is a great book.

Chapter 7

An Appropriate View of Success

*The key to long-term success is a willingness to disrupt
your own comfort for the sake of continued growth.*

—TODD HENRY

R egardless of what they tell you, the goal of all writers is to
be read. To be read by many people and preferably those
who actually buy the books—that's success. As a writer myself, I
love to watch how authors respond when their works take off and
they actually achieve the success they dreamed of when they were
slaving over an overheating laptop computer.

What I've seen is that success does funny things to people,
authors included. Some let the fame go to their heads. Some handle celebrity in stride. Still others go into seclusion and are never
heard from again.

You can tell a lot about a person by the way he or she handles
success.

Our case study for this part of the book is perhaps the most successful writer of all time, at least if we are judging by number of readers. As I mentioned earlier, the apostle Paul wrote the majority of the New Testament portion of the Bible. And the Bible is the most read book in the history of the world.

> *Not the United States.*
> *Not in Europe.*
> *And not in the last century.*
> *In. The. World. Ever!*

In addition to penning two-thirds of the New Testament, Paul was also one of the greatest thought leaders of his day and was responsible for the spread of Christianity to the non-Jewish world, which is basically 99 percent of people on the earth.

So if any writer in history had the right to brag a little bit about his success, it was Paul. And yet what we see in his life is just the opposite. In one of his letters to a group of leaders in a city called Philippi, he wrote the following,

> I could have confidence in my own effort if anyone could. Indeed, if others have reason for confidence in their own efforts, I have even more!

He then went on to describe all his accomplishments, which even then were truly impressive. At point in his life, Paul had achieved the kind of success as a Jewish religious leader that would have made his Jewish readers say, "Holy Moses! This guy is unbelievable." But then, in a powerful twist, Paul made a statement that revealed how he felt about all the impressive things he had done:

> I once thought these things were valuable, but now I consider them worthless because of what Christ has done.[1]

Did you catch that? Paul wrote off every single one of his accomplishments. With one single stroke of the pen he excluded himself from every award show that would ever try to hail him as something special. In one sentence he took the shine off every trophy anyone would ever try to give him.

Paul had a view of his achievements that not only kept him humble but made him one of the most teachable people to ever walk the earth. He understood that one of the greatest enemies of teachability in his life could very well be the thing that he and every one of us desire most.

ONE OF THE GREATEST THREATS TO OUR TEACHABILITY IS SUCCESS.

Success.

THE THREATS OF SUCCESS

Let me say it plainly: one of the greatest threats to our teachability is success.

That's a crazy kind of paradox when you think about it, isn't it? Because the more teachable you are, the more successful you will become. But then the more successful you become, the more you will be in danger of losing your teachability.

Not everything about success is good. In fact, there are three invisible threats built into success that we cannot ignore.

Threat #1: We Will Trust Too Much in Our Natural Abilities and Stop Learning from Others.

Some of the most talented people in the world today are also the most unteachable. This can be seen from the professional sports field to the classroom to the conference room to the living room. But why?

The reason our natural ability can become a liability to our teachability is that it tempts us to depend too much on ourselves. In other words, we start to lean on our own skills, abilities, knowledge, strength, and savvy.

Unfortunately, none of us is born that good.

The truth is, all the talent in the world can never take us to the level of our full potential. Only teachability can do that.

None of us is as good at the beginning as we can be at the end if we will remain teachable. Regardless of what we set out to achieve—to become a great parent, a sales leader, a star athlete, an academic powerhouse, or yes, a bestselling author, we will never know as much at the beginning as we will when we reach the pinnacle of the success we're chasing.

Teachability is the only way to discover how great we can become. And becoming great hinges upon how much we're willing to learn.

Again, Paul is such a great historical example for us. Talk about a guy who was born with natural ability. He was a natural organizer, a charismatic leader, a stellar writer. And he still had those abilities after his life-changing encounter with God, but he didn't put too much stock in them. In fact, he never put much faith or confidence in his own natural ability again.

In the same letter to the Philippians we referenced above, he wrote, "For [Jesus'] sake I have discarded everything else, counting [my successes] as garbage."[2] Paul wanted everyone to know that the success he achieved from his natural ability wasn't worth as much as they thought it was. What mattered was that he remained open and teachable.

That's true for all of us as well. Long-term success will always hinge upon the ability to keep an appropriate view of our natural abilities—to use them well but not depend on them, and most of all to keep on growing and learning.

Threat #2: We Think (or Others Think) We Are Something Special.

It's well known that success changes people. But success also changes perception. It changes the way other people see us and the way they act toward us. It can also change the way we see ourselves. And either can get in the way of our teachability.

The more successful we become, for instance, the more we may have to fight to get accurate information and feedback from the people around us. John Maxwell explains it this way:

> When you are influential and highly respected, people tend to tell you what you want to hear, not what you *need* to hear. They are seeking your approval, or they flatter you. Unfortunately, that creates a gap between what you hear and reality. If you find yourself in that situation, you will need to work extra hard to get the people close to you to speak

honesty into your life. And you will have to become highly intentional in observing and listening."[3]

I know this to be true from my own experience. As our organization reached the ten-year mark and began to take on significance in terms of size and influence, a strange thing started to happen. People started to treat me differently—and not just outside people like other pastors or leaders, but people inside our organization as well, people who had been close to me for years and had even taken the majority of the journey with me. Conversations changed tone when I walked in the room. People acted strangely toward me.

I had not changed, but how I was perceived as a leader had changed because of the success we had achieved. To this day, I have to be very intentional about making sure that people tell me what I need to hear, not just what they think I want to hear. If I let it, the change in their perception can easily get in the way of my teachability.

But it's not just the perception of others that can be a problem when it comes to success. Our perception of ourselves can easily change as well. It's all too easy to start believing our own press, to start thinking we don't have to listen to others around us. Such an attitude can easily sabotage teachability if we are not careful.

Threat #3: We Think That Because We Know Something, We Know it All.

Have you ever heard of "the curse of knowledge"? According to Wikipedia, the term refers to "a cognitive bias that leads better-informed parties to find it extremely difficult to think about problems from the perspective of lesser-informed parties."

Let me put that in layman's terms: the more we know about a subject, the harder it is to receive from those we think know less.

This can be a problem when it comes to teachability. The curse of knowledge can cause us to shut people down, interrupt them, and tune them out. The curse of knowledge works against us because it causes us to make assumptions about what others are going to say and stop listening to what they are actually saying.

Ever been guilty of that? Ever rushed to the end of a story that someone was telling? Ever cut someone off or tried to finish his or her sentence in an effort to somehow speed him or her up? I know I have. But I didn't know I did it until my youngest son, who is just like me, started doing it to me.

> **THE MORE WE KNOW ABOUT A SUBJECT, THE HARDER IT IS TO RECEIVE FROM THOSE WE THINK KNOW LESS.**

I'd be telling a story, and he'd give away the punch line before it was time. After one such instance where this had happened, I sat him down to show him what he had been doing—then suddenly realized he had learned it from me. In the weeks following, I became extremely aware of this shortcoming and worked to improve on it. So did he, by the way.

SAFEGUARDING YOUR TEACHABILITY

So what about you? Are you allowing your own success to diminish your teachability by succumbing to one of the three threats that come with success?

Are you allowing your natural ability to give you a license to not pay attention and learn from others? Are you using your previous success to shield you from being open to learning something new from a colleague? Have you taken your current level of success and seen it as the reason why you didn't need to stay open and teachable?

Having identified these three threats, let me give you what I know you're hoping would come next, and that is: the three remedies to these things. After all, if the fruit of teachability in your life is greater success, but greater success has the power to rob you of greater teachability, then how do you handle success when it comes in order to keep growing into ever greater success? In the remainder of the chapter, I want to offer you three remedies to help you keep a healthy perspective on success when it comes your way and remain teachable despite your level of success.

Remedy #1: Be More Concerned About "Our" Success Than About "Your" Success.

A mind-set that says, "I never succeed alone" will position you to not allow your success to go to your head. After all, if you didn't win by yourself, then you can't take all the credit.

From the time we founded our organization in 2002, I have always made it my aim to use "we" and "us" language rather than "I" language when referring to what we do. I want inclusive language to define the culture of who we are. Whenever there is a success to be celebrated, I always think of it as "our win" not just "my win." I have tried to model this in my language, in my tone, and in my approach to success whenever it comes our way.

What is interesting is that today, when I am around people

who use "I" exclusively to describe what is happening in their organization, it instantly sticks out to me. I can't help but wonder if they would get greater buy-in from their team if they made a simple switch from "I" and "me" to "us" and "we."

What about you? Do you tend to take the credit or give the credit when success comes your way? What would your co-workers say about that? Would your team members agree with your assessment?

Remedy #2: Be Generous in Your Success.

One of the tricky things about success in life is that it usually brings with it increase as well—financial increase, increased recognition, or some other perk. One of the greatest ways to maintain your teachability in the midst of success is to recognize that this bounty is not just for you. Whenever an increase comes your way, don't keep it all for yourself. Instead share it with others, even give a portion of it away. Don't keep it all for yourself.

How generous are you in your success? What would your friends say? When increase comes your way, do you think of yourself or others first?

I believe you'll find that being generous opens up compartments of your heart that can't be opened any other way. In this way, generosity actually becomes a catalyst for growth.

Remedy #3: Recognize That Success Is Fragile and Temporary.

It's kind of weird to say, but in one hundred years nobody will know who you and I were. Think about it for a second. On this date one hundred years in the future, unless you are the president of the United States, nobody will remember you.[4]

Now, before you sink into a sullen depression at that thought, stay with me for a minute. Here's the point. When it comes to success, everything we achieve could be gone tomorrow. Even if we are the new hot thing in our industry right now, there's a good chance that in ten or fifteen years, tops, we'll be the "remember that one thing from a long time ago?" Even the biggest events in history eventually become yesterday's news. So, too, the success that makes us think we are something special right now won't last forever.

All this means that it's not wise to hold success too tightly. Be grateful for it. Be generous with it, and you will probably get to experience more of it. But keep in mind how fleeting any success is, and don't be tempted to believe it will last forever.

Closing Thoughts on Success

Success affects all of us differently, but one thing is for sure: success will threaten our teachability like few other things will. Wise is the person who is proactive in his or her approach to success before, during, and after it comes his or her way.

If you can remain open, humble, and teachable in the midst of your success, that's when you will truly have succeeded.

NOTES

1. The Bible passage I quote throughout this chapter is Philippians 3:4–8 NLT.
2. Philippians 3:8 NLT.
3. John Maxwell, *Sometimes You Win—Sometimes You Learn: Life's Greatest Lessons Are Gained from Our Losses* (New York: Center Street/Hachette, 2013), 117.
4. If you *are* the president of the United States and you're reading this—I

am freaking out right now. But seriously, I am honored, and I would love to help you any way I can. I definitely have some ideas on how to make better leaders in America. Call me. I can come to you. No need to bring *Air Force One* all the way down here to Florida!

Chapter 8

An Openness to Feedback

A teachable spirit is a teachable spirit regardless of the teacher.

—TODD MULLINS

A friend of mine set out to open a new franchise several years ago. He was convinced that was what he was supposed to do. He had a lot of experience working for others in the industry but he had never been the main guy. He also knew the industry had changed a lot since he had first joined it more than twenty years earlier. But he was ready. He was confident he had what it took to succeed.

He went through the application and interview process and passed with flying colors. His next step was to attend the week-long training event at the headquarters of the franchise company. And that is where his teachability test began.

When he arrived for the opening day of training, he realized that everyone being trained to open a new franchise was fifteen to twenty years younger than he was. This was no call-your-wife-and-tell-her-you're-like-the-oldest-guy-in-the-class-but-it's-okay-because-it's-only-by-like-five-years-at-the-most situation.[1] No, this was more like a try-not-to-freak-out-because-man-these-jokers-look-like-they-could-be-my-kids situation.

My friend told me that the first two days of the training were a bit of a soul crisis for him. First, there was the sheer intimidation of being the "old guy" in the room. *Am I doing the right thing? Am I too old to be doing this? Is this even wise? Am I being delusional in thinking I could actually pull off something like this?* But then came the realization that these "kids" knew a lot about the market that he didn't know. They were ahead of the game and he actually had a lot to learn from them.

My friend's teachability test came in deciding whether he would allow the young entrepreneurs around him to give him the feedback he needed in order to be successful, or would he choose to close himself off to them simply because they were younger.

> TEACHABLE PEOPLE SEE FEEDBACK AS THEIR FRIEND—THEIR BEST FRIEND.

Thankfully, he chose to make his competition his allies. Today my friend runs one of the most successful franchises in that industry in all of the southeastern United States. And all because he chose teachability.

CHOOSING FEEDBACK

One of the leading characteristics of the most teachable people in the world is that they don't just tolerate feedback, they welcome it. Teachable people see feedback as their friend—their best friend. They understand that the only way to become everything they were created to be is by developing a lifestyle where feedback is constant, welcomed, and sought after.

John Maxwell says, "Be willing to accept feedback and criticism without defending yourself. Otherwise, you'll only receive it once."[2] If we're going to adopt a lifestyle of teachability, then we must take a proper approach to feedback.

MUTUAL SUBMISSION

Our case study from the first century, Paul, not only knew how to give feedback, but he knew how to take it as well. A great illustration of this is found in chapter 15 of the book of Acts, where much of the detail of Paul's leadership journey is recorded.

Paul and his partner Barnabas had been taking the message of Jesus outside the predictable circles of the Jewish community to the non-Jews, also known as Gentiles. And many influential Jewish Christians were all up in arms about what was going on. There had been some pretty heated debates over these issues. So a big conference was called in Jerusalem to discuss the issues that had arisen with these new missionary efforts.

When Paul and Barnabas began to share with the big dogs—that is, the "apostles and elders" in Jerusalem—about how people's lives were being changed outside of the Jewish community, nobody could argue that this was a good thing. But the situation did raise a really big—and very tricky—question.

Up to this point, you see, all the people who had become Christians had been Jews like Jesus and His disciples. So when non-Jewish people responded to a message that came from the Jewish tradition, did they have to adopt all of the Jewish laws and customs as well?

More specifically, they wanted to know if male Gentiles who became Christians had to be . . . eh . . . well . . . um . . . how do I say this . . . circumcised?[3]

Yep, you heard me right. The debate was over whether or not the Gentile guys would have to become Jews in order to be Christians. And to become Jews they would have to—well, you know. I know what Paul must have been thinking: *If that's a requirement, then that's going to seriously affect our conversion rates.*

Long story short, they had the meeting, everybody weighed in, and then James, who was the acting pastor (or CEO, to use a business term) of the church and council at Jerusalem, delivered the verdict: "It is my judgment, therefore, that we should not make it difficult for the Gentiles who are turning to God."[4] In other words, "Guys, let's not make it any harder than it needs to be for people who want to follow Jesus." Which, as you can imagine, was good news for all the Gentiles who were listening in on the conference-call line, right? Paul and Barnabas submitted to the council and headed off with their detailed marching orders straight from headquarters.

Now, here's where the teachability piece kicks in. I believe that no matter what verdict came down from headquarters that day, Paul and Barnabas would have submitted to it. Why do I think that? Because they were willing to travel all the way to Jerusalem to get advice from the apostles and elders. That's what teachable people do; they invite and embrace feedback. And we have no evidence that Paul and Barnabas bucked against the council's decision or pushed back in any way. They remained open and teachable, and consequently, when they got back to their territory, their message spread farther and faster than it ever had previously.

Our openness to feedback is the great multiplier to our teachability. In the remainder of this chapter, I want to suggest four ways to approach feedback and improve your teachability.

Feedback Strategy #1: Listen to Others Who May Not Be at Your Level.

To increase your teachability, you must be willing to receive feedback even from people you think may not be at your level. As you heard in my friend's story at the beginning of the chapter, this can be difficult, but that doesn't make it wrong or ineffective. My friend's success was directly proportional to his willingness to learn from anybody, anywhere, anytime.

As a sports enthusiast, I enjoy watching golf on the weekends, and now that my youngest son is playing, I enjoy it even more.[5] As a student of leadership and teachability, I am always fascinated by the interaction that takes place between a professional golfer and his caddie. Several times in a weekend, you will see a golfer and a caddie have a heated debate about club selection on a tee box.

For me, this is one of the most incredible examples of teachability anywhere, because the golfer is the one with his reputation on the line. He's the one with everything to lose. He's the one who actually has to swing the club and live with the consequences.

The caddie, on the other hand, is the guy who enjoyed playing golf growing up and maybe even played at a moderate level in college. Clearly he wasn't good enough to play professionally. If he was, well, he would be the guy playing golf instead of the one carrying the clubs. The caddie has nothing to lose—except his job, I guess, but his name and reputation are not on the line. And yet time and again you will see a professional golfer submit to his caddie on the course. Even though his caddie isn't on the same level in terms of skill, the golfer gives him permission to give him real-time feedback that the golfer knows can make him better in the moment.

How many people do you have in your world whom you have invited to give that kind of real-time feedback? That's what teachable people do. They don't pretend to be able to see every situation from every angle. And they are more than willing to invite others into their world, even others at a lower level, to help them see things more clearly.

If you're a leader of a department or company, you can benefit from seeking your subordinates' feedback. If you're a singer or musician, you need people to help you listen better—even if those people may not be able to play as well as you. If you're an athlete, you need your teammates to help you see what you can't see to improve your game. Feedback is an essential friend for anyone who wants to improve their teachability.

Receiving Feedback Strategy #2: Cultivate an Appropriate Response to Feedback.

To improve your teachability, you must approach feedback differently than other people. Author Seth Godin says, "If you're afraid of . . . feedback, it's probably not going to arrive as often as you'd like it to. On the other hand, if you embrace it as the gift it can be, you may decide to go looking for it."[6]

Most people tend to entertain feedback with a closed mind, a clinched jaw, and a skeptical spirit. But not teachable people.

They take an entirely different approach, and that proves to be the difference maker in their growth on the back end. The next time someone gives you feedback, try to remember the following five tips for responding to feedback more effectively.

1. *Put yourself in the other person's shoes.* Recognize how hard it must be to be the person having to give this feedback to you—especially if that person is a subordinate. Think about the last time you chose to give someone feedback. It wasn't easy, was it? Letting people know that you know how hard this must be for them will up the likelihood that they'll tell you more of what you need to hear.

2. *Manage your countenance.* This is something my wife tells me I need to work on with my kids. I'm the kind of guy who wears my emotions on my sleeve, which can be a good thing and a bad thing. It's good because you always know where you stand with me, but it's bad because I'm not very good at "putting on a happy face." So sometimes my face gives away what I'm thinking and, consequently, my kids shut down and stop talking. (I'm working on this.) When someone gives you feedback, be extremely aware of how you appear to him or her. What facial expression and body language are you showing? Are your arms crossed? Are you wringing your hands? All these subtle clues either help or hinder the feedback you are receiving and affect the level of feedback you'll receive in the future.

3. *Refuse to get defensive, no matter what is said.* Even if someone tells you something that is hard to hear, refuse to fight back. Don't be thinking about comebacks or excuses. Just listen. Getting defensive while receiving feedback is one of

the surest ways to guarantee that the person giving it will never do so again. And feedback is what you need to reach your full potential, remember? The words of Joseph Flom can be helpful here: "You should recognize that criticism is not always a put down. If you take it to heart, maybe it will guide the way you ought to be going."[7]

4. *Ask questions if the person giving feedback seems apprehensive or hesitant to share details.* Don't hesitate to ask for clarification if there are things you don't see right away or understand. Your willingness to ask questions will confirm to the other person that you really are interested in what he or she has to say.

5. *Don't write off feedback from people you don't happen to like.* Some of the best feedback I've ever gotten has come from some of my least favorite people. If you find it difficult to separate the message from the messenger, try thinking to yourself, *If this was coming from my best friend, how open to hearing it would I be?* Then decide to be that open to them in the moment. Feedback is one of the most powerful tools you have to improve your teachability, but only if you know how to receive it.

Receiving Feedback Strategy #3: Be Willing to Receive Feedback Even When You Don't Like How It's Being Delivered.

You will get the most out of feedback when you are willing to receive it regardless of how it is delivered. Listen, just because the guy delivering your pizza hasn't showered in a week, drives a beater car that you can hear coming a mile away, and looks like he shouldn't be left alone with small children—that doesn't mean the pizza isn't delicious.[8]

Sometimes the best feedback is delivered in a way that hurts us or offends us. Don't discount any feedback simply because it comes in an unpleasant form.

Receiving Feedback Strategy #4: Don't Just Take Feedback When it Comes. Ask for It.

Many people hesitate to come right out and ask for feedback. They rarely ask, "What do you think?" or "What would you do if you were me?" Instead, they make a mentor, boss, or friend stick their foot in the door and force their way in if they want to offer feedback.

One of the greatest things you can learn concerning feedback is this principle: don't make the other person do the hard work to make you better. Specifically, invite the opinions of people you trust, and make it easy for them to share those opinions.

DON'T MAKE THE OTHER PERSON DO THE HARD WORK TO MAKE YOU BETTER.

The thing to remember is that you need feedback from others more than they need to give it—which means, if you don't ask for it, they probably won't give it! And if they don't give it, you probably won't get where you want to go.

The best and only choice concerning feedback is to invite it early, often, and all the time—and then be extremely teachable in the process. The harder you make it for the people in your life to give you feedback, the less of it you will receive. But the easier you make it for the people around you to give you feedback, the more of it you will receive. Don't miss that!

Receiving feedback is a choice—a choice that can make all the difference in your life. Looking back over my life, I can see that the times when I dared to ask someone for their feedback were the times when I grew the most in the shortest amount of time. Inviting feedback is the great expediter of your teachability.

NOTES

1. Come on, everyone who's in their forties now. (You know what I mean.)
2. Maxwell, *Sometimes You Win—Sometimes You Learn*, 117.
3. Ouch. Simply, ouch.
4. This is a direct quote from Acts 15:19. You should read the whole story if you have time.
5. I'm not saying I am any good at playing golf, but I certainly enjoy being outdoors and hanging out in a beautiful setting. So if you want to take me golfing sometime, I won't say no.
6. I highly recommend Seth Godin's daily blog on marketing and leadership at www.SethGodin.com. The quote in the chapter came from his January 11, 2014, blog post. Here's the link: http://sethgodin.typepad.com/seths_blog/2014/01/the-feedback-youve-been-waiting-for.html.
7. Joseph H. Flom, "No Magic Formula," in *Letters from Leaders: Personal Advice for Tomorrow's Leaders from the World's Most Influential People* (Guilford, CT: Lyons Press, 2009), 72.
8. Come on, pizza places that deliver. You really should at least start making these guys shower regularly.

Chapter 9

A Flexible Approach to Life

*We cannot change what we are unaware of, and
once we are aware, we cannot help but change.*

— SHERYL SANDBERG

D ictionary.com defines the word *flexible* as "capable of being
bent, usually without breaking." The word can apply to
physical things like bendy straws or rubber tubing or yoga instruc-
tors' spines, but it also describes a kind of attitude and outlook.
And teachable people are inherently flexible in their approach to
life. Unteachable people, by contrast, tend to be rigid, stiff, and
stuck in their ways.

You might say, in fact, that teachability gives us *agility* to
exceed our ability.[1]

A TEACHABILITY CROSSROADS

In the fall of 1997, the San Antonio Spurs took a six-foot-eleven
center as their number-one draft pick. He came from Wake Forest

University, and his name was Tim Duncan. The basketball world was very high on that young man's potential.

There was no argument that his future with the Spurs looked bright. There was just one problem. The Spurs already had a big man, and he was pretty good. His name was David Robinson.

For eight years, David Robinson had been the seven-foot-one starting center for San Antonio. Night in and night out, he'd owned the "paint" under the basket, and everybody liked it that way. But on October 31, 1997, after more than five hundred games for the Spurs, Robinson's territory was being threatened. The future had arrived in San Antonio, and his name was Tim Duncan. Duncan, the rookie, would start alongside Robinson, the veteran. The young college hotshot would now compete for playing time with the veteran star.

At this point, David Robinson had a choice to make. He was at a teachability crossroads. Would he become defensive and territorial and try and keep Duncan down? Or would he adjust, be flexible, and do what was best for the team?

Robinson chose the latter, and the results speak for themselves. Though Robinson's playing time went down, the team's winning percentage went up. In the eight seasons leading up to the 1997–98 season, with the exception of one season when he was hurt, Robinson had averaged thirty-eight minutes of playing time per game. In the seven seasons after Duncan arrived, he averaged just over thirty. But, in the eight seasons leading up to the arrival of Duncan, the San Antonio Spurs had won a total of zero championships. In the seven years they played together, the Spurs won two championships.

What was the key to their success? David Robinson was teachable and flexible. His willingness to be flexible in the face of change created a culture that set the stage for years of winning in San Antonio.[2]

SOME TIPS FOR FLEXIBILITY

Now, you might not be a seven-foot professional basketball player, but I can guarantee that you will find yourself at a similar crossroads at times in your life. When faced with a challenge or change, you must choose between bristling or bending, being adamant or adaptive. The choice to be flexible is almost always the teachable choice. The following suggestions can help you be more flexible.

Flexibility Tip #1: Be Willing to Adapt.

If there's one guarantee in life, it's that change is inevitable.[3] An unwillingness to adapt to that change will keep you from being as successful as you can be. However, being teachable enough to go with the flow of change will help you win.

Growing up, I was an Indiana Hoosiers basketball fan, and I always found it interesting to watch the influx of new freshmen to the team. Each fall brought with it a new set of high-school standouts, each of whom had been the star of his hometown team. But playing college ball at Indiana would mean these new Hoosiers would need to adapt to a new system, a new approach to the game, and a new way of thinking. Their success or failure at the collegiate level inevitably hinged upon their willingness to adapt. Year in and year out, the players who embraced an attitude of teachability and adapted to the new program succeeded, while those who refused to be flexible struggled.

What's true of college athletes is also true of you and me. Success and failure in any area of life rises and falls on our ability to adapt to new circumstances.

If you're a new husband and you're still trying to act like you're single—trust me, you're in trouble.

If you're newly hired in the marketing division but you aren't willing to listen to how things are done at your new company— you're going to struggle.

If you're an executive who just got promoted to oversee fifty employees and you try to lead the way you led a small handful of people previously, you're setting yourself up to fail.

In all these cases, flexibility in the face of change is the only way to succeed. We've got to master the art of bending without breaking. John Maxwell said it best when he said, "If you want to keep leading, you must keep learning. Yesterday's growth cannot suffice for today. We must remain teachable and flexible."[4]

Flexibility Tip #2: Refuse to Become Set in Your Ways.

As we talked about in the chapter on how to handle success, the more successful we become, the more difficult teachability can become. One of the biggest reasons for this is that success tempts us to get comfortable and set in our ways. John Maxwell describes this dangerous mindset: "Leaders face the danger of contentment with the status quo. After all, if a leader already possesses influence and has achieved a level of respect, why should he or she keep growing?"[5]

The reason, of course, is that if we don't respond to change, change will pass us by. This is true not only of individuals, but of businesses, teams, and even entire industries. In our new global, connected world, the speed of change is increasing by the minute. Information is being transferred at lightning speed, and opportunities seem to emerge just as quickly. Responding to these changes requires a flexible outlook and a willingness to adapt and grow.

Too many leaders and organizations have failed to recognize this reality. They continue to do business the way it has always been done, hoping they'll get the results they've always gotten. This is delusional thinking in today's fast-paced world. Sadly, many established companies are being passed by and swallowed up—all because the leaders have been unwilling to adapt and be teachable.

Nearly every area of endeavor in our country is being affected by this dynamic—from the auto industry to the housing market to cameras and GPS units to publishing—even faith and family life. Life is happening at the speed of change, and individuals and organizations that don't respond with flexibility are being left behind.

Our case study on teachability, Paul, shared some wisdom related to this subject in a letter he wrote to a group of leaders he was mentoring in the city of Philippi. "Not that I have already . . . arrived at my goal," he wrote, "but I press on to take hold of that for which Christ Jesus took hold of me."[6] In other words, Paul was saying, "I haven't arrived yet. Yes, I've come a long way, but there's still more ahead for me. And I'm not going to stop changing and adapting until I get where I'm going."

What about you? Have you become rigid or resistant in some area of your life? Is there some area where you are stuck and rigid instead of flexible and adaptable? How proactive are you toward trying new approaches? Are you actively pursuing the future or just dealing with it haphazardly as it comes? What effort and attention are you putting into adapting and changing with the times? Remaining set in our ways is not an option if we desire to succeed in the future.

Flexibility Tip #3: Don't Freak Out About a Lateral Move.

It's just a fact that not everything we do is going to propel us forward. Sometimes life moves us sideways or even backward. One of the most difficult transition seasons you will ever go through in your career is when you are demoted, moved laterally, or fired. In your personal life there may be an unwelcomed or unexpected move, a family upheaval, or a change in circumstances that leaves you feeling like you've lost ground. In these moments your pride and ego are likely to raise their ugly heads and tempt you to dig in and resist instead of adapt.

Being flexible means learning to take these seasons in stride. People with high teachability know that even when change seems bad or neutral at best, there is much to be learned in it.

I recently had a friend make a really profound statement while we were talking about this concept. He said, "Teachable people don't get discouraged by lateral moves or even setbacks. They simply see them as another opportunity to learn from a different seat on the bus."

Gabe Bedenbaugh is one of the bright young leaders in our organization. In his short four-year tenure on our staff, he has served in a half-dozen different positions. When we first hired him, he oversaw our entire hospitality team, which included more than 150 volunteers that needed to be trained, coached, inspired, scheduled, and led every week. After a few months we moved Gabe over our outreach and connection-groups departments, which meant he needed to learn three hundred new names, faces, and stories in order to lead these two teams effectively. Then about two years ago, we moved Gabe into the role of leading our entire production department, where he now oversees all of the video, audio, lighting, recording, and broadcasting technicalities for both locations of our church—a huge responsibility.

At any point over the past several years, Gabe could have decided he wasn't interested in moving to a new seat on the bus. But he didn't do that. Instead he embraced teachability, and today he is excelling in his leadership and does a phenomenal job overseeing his teams and fulfilling his own responsibilities. Rather than view those lateral moves as obstacles or setbacks, Gabe chose to be flexible. He decided to love the bus more than his seat on the bus and consequently has become a great asset to our organization.

The best-case scenario for you when you find yourself having to make a lateral or downward move is to remain flexible. Keep your head up and go with the flow while keeping your ultimate goals in mind. What looks like a sideways move right now might just be leading you to your greater mission. Besides, if you sacrifice your flexibility, you may forfeit a great opportunity to learn something about yourself that you didn't know before.

BENDABLE—AND TEACHABLE

As we said at the beginning of the chapter, the word *flexible* means "capable of being bent, usually without breaking." And that's actually the point, isn't it? When we allow ourselves to bend, we're not likely to break.

That doesn't mean we become spineless or wishy-washy,

though. It doesn't mean we give up our goals or compromise our convictions or never take a stand. Some issues will always require standing firm instead of bending. But not all issues! When we keep our eyes on what is most important and remain open to new possibilities and approaches, we actually grow more stable and resilient, not less.

Bend without breaking—that not only sounds like flexibility; it sounds like teachability too. And it's the optimal approach to a rapidly changing future.

NOTES

1. Sorry about the rhyming there. I just figured that this far into the book, we know each other well enough to be a little cheesy. I won't let that happen again.
2. As recently as 2014, the Spurs once again made it to the NBA Finals, where they defeated the Miami Heat and collected their fourth title in fourteen years.
3. I was going to use that old cliché, "The only constant in life is change," but I promised you I wouldn't throw in any more cheesy one-liners. You're welcome.
4. John C. Maxwell, "Teachability: To Keep Leading, Keep Learning" (commentary on Jeremiah 18:18), in *The Maxwell Leadership Bible: Lessons in Leadership from the Word of God, New International Version* (Nashville: Thomas Nelson, 2014), 895.
5. Maxwell, "Teachability: Apollos Learned and Grew" (commentary on Acts 18:24–28), in *The Maxwell Leadership Bible, NIV,* 1323.
6. This verse of the Bible is found in Philippians 3:12.

Chapter 10

An Ability to Handle Failure Well

*To be wrong as fast as you can is to sign
up for aggressive, rapid learning.*

—ED CATMULL

In 1983, Apple Computers, Inc. was still a young company. Steve Jobs was a twenty-eight-year-old idea generator with more ideas than leadership skill and wisdom. Fresh off the success of the Apple IIe computer, which now filled school classrooms across the country, Steve and Apple pursued what they believed to be the next great advancement in computer technology. It was affectionately named after Steve's daughter—Lisa.

Unfortunately, the computer didn't live up to its cute name. With an asking price of ten thousand dollars per unit[1] and $150 million in development cost, Lisa crashed and burned. In fact, some rumors circulated at the time that Apple had literally taken the remaining stock and buried it in a landfill in Logan, Utah.

Yes, Apple failed. In a big way.

Though we remember Steve Jobs today as a world-changing mind, he was also a man who had some pretty big swing-and-misses in his career, the Lisa included. But Steve Jobs never let failure destroy him. Instead, he became known for picking himself up after every knockdown and rising up again. His example is an important one, because knowing how to handle failure well is essential to growing your teachability.

A Different Kind of Failure

Our case study on teachability in this part of the book, the apostle Paul, endured failure of a different kind. He didn't make a mistake or a misjudgment. He didn't do anything wrong. But still he had failure thrust upon him.

Paul had to endure some of the most horrendous forms of mistreatment known to man simply because some people in his culture found his message offensive. He was beaten multiple times within an inch of his life, imprisoned repeatedly, and even sentenced to death. And because of these bad things that happened to him, his planned missions did not always go as planned.

Yet when you study Paul's writings, you don't see a man who let failure and misfortune keep him down. Through it all, Paul kept his heart right and handled his mistreatment with courage and perseverance. In a letter to one of his protégés, he wrote, "I am willing to endure anything."[2]

What a perspective from a man who could have chosen to become jaded, cynical, bitter, or worse. In light of all that happened to him, Paul might have been justified in giving in to failure. Instead he kept on striving toward his goals.

FAILURE . . . AN INEVITABILITY

Let me say this as plainly as I can. Failure is going to happen to you. You may have dedicated your life to making sure it doesn't happen—but it will. It may happen because of a misjudgment or mistake on your part—like Steve Jobs' failure with the Lisa. Or it may result from someone else's actions—like Paul's failure. But it will happen. No one is exempt from facing failure, and experiencing failure can really do a number on us if we're not prepared for it.

First, *failure shakes our confidence.* Where we once walked into a meeting and knew exactly what we wanted to say and wanted to see accomplished, failure can make us timid. Where once conversation flowed freely among team members, a failure of some kind can make everyone sheepish and nervous. Failure can turn those who once were the life of the party into wallflowers and recluses. And the failure doesn't have to be big for this to happen. I have seen some of the most outwardly successful people in their fields get rattled by a seemingly miniscule misstep.

Second, *failure tends to reveal our true selves.* One of the scariest things about failure is that it forces us to come face-to-face with who we really are. Whereas success generates a great-looking mask we can hide behind, failure rips that mask off. There's nothing like failure to shine the harsh light of reality on our lives.

Third, *failure can cause us to question everything.* When things are going well, the assumptions we make about our careers, our relationships, and our lives in general stay firmly intact. After all, they're working for us, right? But when we experience failure, that's when we start wondering. Some of the most unsettling times I have ever faced have come in the days following a failure of some kind. Fear and doubt hide in the back pockets of failure and can threaten our joy, our confidence, and our very sense of self.

THE HIDDEN PERK OF FAILURE

Failure is never a pleasant experience. Sometimes it's downright awful. And yet there's a plus side to failure, because it can be the fastest way to learn. Pixar Studios president Ed Catmull stated this memorably in his book, *Creativity, Inc.*: "To be wrong as fast as you can is to sign up for aggressive, rapid learning."[3]

People with high teachability take advantage of this "perk" of failure. Instead of letting themselves become cynical or depressed, they lean in to the failure as quickly as they can and search for the lessons. The following three strategies can help you do this when you face a failure situation of some kind in your life.

Failure Strategy #1: Turn the Spotlight on Yourself.

John Maxwell is famous for saying that "experience is not the best teacher—examined experience is."[4] That statement is never truer than when we are dealing with failure.

The next time you fail, instead of pointing the finger at others, allow the spotlight to be turned on you. Don't spend your time—or, more accurately, waste your time—blaming others or making excuses. Instead, use the situation as an opportunity for self-reflection.

A couple of years ago, when my youngest son, Drew, was ten years old, he got in trouble at school. In the grand scheme of things, what he did was not a big deal. At the time, however, the experience hit him pretty hard. We dealt with the situation, he apologized to the affected parties, and life moved on. But when I started writing this chapter, I asked him about that event and what he had learned. "I don't want to talk about the mistakes, Dad," he said. "But those are the things that have taught me the most."

Of course, as a dad, I was falling all over myself at the cuteness of that statement. But as an author and speaker, I was thinking, *I've got to write this down because that's awesome.* If my ten-year-old could understand what it means to learn from failure, then so can you and I.

SOME OF LIFE'S GREATEST LESSONS ARE ON SALE TO US IN THE MIDST OF OUR FAILURES.

There's a simple mantra when it comes to investing that states, "Buy low, sell high." Every financial advisor knows the way to create the most value is to pay as small of a price as you can and then hold on to that investment for maximum value. Some of life's greatest lessons are on sale to us in the midst of our failures. When you stop and examine a failed experience to learn all you can, you are essentially buying some of life's greatest lessons at the lowest possible price. If you don't learn all you can from your mistakes, then you are signing up to pay a much higher price in the future by repeating them.

So let's make this personal for a minute. When was the last time you stopped in a failure situation and examined why it went wrong and what you could learn from what was happening? This takes us back to the Desire-to-Learn-times-Willingness-to-Change formula again. When you face failure in your life, either small or great, how great is your desire to learn from it?

I get that being open and teachable in the middle of a painful failure is extremely difficult. It's hard to swallow our pride and admit we screwed up. It is no fun to raise our hands and admit our failures. But in order for us to reach our full potential, we have to learn that skill.

What if the failure wasn't your fault? What if, like Paul, your failure is due largely to someone else's mistakes or even malice? Even in cases like that, self-examination is an important part of responding to the problem.

For one thing, chances are that you *did* contribute to the failure in some way—a rash decision, an unwise response, something. But even if you were totally blameless, taking the time to assess what happened and why can build your confidence and help you to avoid repeats of the situation.

Failure Strategy #2: Refuse to Rush Past a Failure.

Failure is uncomfortable, so it's always tempting to "move on" as quickly as we can. But what I've come to learn over the course of my life is that it's much better to slow down, face the situation fully, and own my part in the failure. I don't like admitting my mistakes any more than you do, but I have come to realize that the minute I stop trying to cover them up or gloss over them, the better things get—and ironically, when I slow down and face an error, I actually seem to get past it sooner.

Most of the time, I find the failure is never as bad as it seems. There are very few disasters that can't be mitigated to some degree by a humble attitude and teachable spirit.

Additionally, when I stop and take responsibility for a failure, I instantly get to move from blame or suspicion mode to learning mode. Dissecting a problem in order to learn is way better than dissecting a problem in order to find fault and lay blame.

To grow your teachability, take the time to really own your failures instead of just rushing by them as fast as you can. Force yourself to slow down and extract every ounce of learning from your experience that you possibly can. If you can manage to do that, you will get the most value out of your failures.

Failure Strategy #3: Don't Let Failure Define You.

We've all seen it—and it's always tragic. A person of tremendous potential makes a big mistake and somehow never gets past the failure.

The great athlete who had the world at his fingertips makes a dumb mistake and never manages to live it down.

The powerful leader whose career was on the rise had a temporary lapse in judgment, then seemingly fell off the face of the earth.

The public figure who is brought down by a single indiscretion, the teenager whose future is ruined by a youthful mistake—some people endure a time of hardship and are never the same again. It is as if something got lost in the season of failure, and they were never able to find it again. They let their failure define them and were never able to rise above it.

The greatest asset you can possess when it comes to handling failure is the refusal to let that failure permanently define you. This is a choice you can make—to admit your failings honestly and then look past them to see your possibilities. Failure is painful, but it doesn't have to be final. You can find a way to rise up from defeat. You can move on from failure.

That's not to say it's easy or that it will happen quickly. And it's not to say the impact of your failure is trivial.

THE GREATEST ASSET YOU CAN POSSESS WHEN IT COMES TO HANDLING FAILURE IS THE REFUSAL TO LET THAT FAILURE PERMANENTLY DEFINE YOU.

Let me speak candidly to some of you who have suffered some big failures in your past. It is true that some failures leave permanent scars, some inwardly to our hearts and some outwardly to our reputations. Just because a failure has disqualified you in one arena does not mean you are disqualified in every arena. You must keep striving, keep trying, and find another way. Sure, life may never be the same. But different isn't necessarily bad—it's just different.

Some of the people who are impacting our world in a great way today endured unexpected and unwanted detours. Some failed again and again. But they didn't let those failures stop them from achieving greatness anyway.

In the church I lead, we have more than a hundred musicians and singers who use their talents to lead our church in worship each week. One of those singers is a thirty-year-old mom named Tiffany. To me, Tiffany is a shining example of what happens when a person refuses to let failure define her.

Six or seven years ago, Tiffany's life looked completely different than it looks today. She spent three long years throwing herself into a scene that came with bad choices and rough consequences. However, Tiffany didn't let those missteps damage her or define her permanently. Instead, she learned from her mistakes. She put herself through nursing school entirely on her own, and just recently, she resigned from her nursing career and joined the staff of our church to work in our kids' ministry! She continues to use her gifts and talents as a singer and worship leader as well. Her life touches the lives of thousands of people every single week.

As I have observed Tiffany's journey over the past half-decade, there is one word that defines her: *teachable*. Tiffany's teachability gave her the ability not to allow her failures to define her but instead to rise up out of them and achieve the greatness hidden inside her.

The same can be true of you. I don't know the failure you have faced in your life, but I do know that failure is never permanent. Your life after a failure may not look like you had hoped it would look, but that doesn't mean your life is over.

If you've got breath, then there's hope for you. If your heart is still beating, then you still have the ability to rise up out of your failure and become the person you were created to become. It will require teachability and a conscious choice on your part, but you can do it.

I know it's cliché, but it's true: failure is only final if you let it be.

NOTES

1. That's like twenty-two thousand dollars in our money today. Now, that's a crazy expensive computer!

---

2. He wrote this in a letter to one of his apprentices named Timothy. The official Bible reference is 2 Timothy 2:10 NLT.

3. Ed Catmull with Amy Wallace, *Creativity, Inc.: Overcoming the Unseen Forces That Stand in the Way of True Inspiration* (New York: Random House, 2014), 109.

4. John Maxwell.

Part 3

Developing a Lifestyle of Teachability

Your teach-ability determines your use-ability.

—TODD MULLINS

You probably couldn't tell by looking at me, but—how do I say this modestly?—I work out.

Now, here's the deal. I'm not a big lift-weights-so-I-can-look-all-buff-in-the-mirror type of guy. Not that there's anything wrong with that. In fact, if that's your thing, then by all means, I want you to be my friend. But I'm not really into that kind of workout. Honestly, it just seems like a lot of work, and I already have a beautiful wife, and I prefer getting more bang for my buck when I'm in the gym. For me that means the treadmill. Here's why.

First, speaking as much as I do, I need my cardio to be in shape way more than my muscles to be strong.[1]

Second, I love looking down from my nine-inch treadmill perch on all the other lesser worker-outers.[2]

And third, when I'm on the treadmill, I can multitask. In fact, I have found I can actually get a lot of work done while I'm working out. Gives a whole new meaning to the phrase, "I'm working on it," doesn't it?

All joking aside, getting in shape is a lot like developing teachability, in that it's not a one-time thing you do and then you're done. It would be crazy for me to go to the gym one time, walk on the treadmill for forty-five minutes, and then think I'm fit. Physical fitness doesn't happen that way and neither does teachability. Teachability is not something we can develop from a single session or a simple intention. It doesn't develop in spurts and starts. True teachability is a lifestyle—and it takes practice. So in this final part of the book, we are going to look at the five über-practical steps to developing a lifestyle of teachability.[3]

Now, here's what you might be thinking as you read these last chapters: *Seriously, these five things seem so simple! Can this really be all there is to it?* To which I would answer no. There's a *lot* more to teachability than I can cover in these few pages. But these essentials will take you a long, long way on your teachability journey, and without them, you won't get far. If you will implement these five steps, you will be well on your way to developing a lifestyle of teachability that will position you to discover everything else you need to reach your full potential.

NOTES

1. That's what scrawny guys like me tell ourselves anyway.
2. Just kidding, strong guys!
3. Yeah, I'm totally using the dots over the letter *u*—technically called an umlaut—every time I use the prefix *über*. I consider it a bit of a tribute to my German heritage—and Germany did win the World Cup in 2014, by the way.

Chapter 11

Determine How You're Going to Define *Teacher* Forever

Real teachability doesn't limit who we learn
from. Real teachability says, "I'll learn anything,
anytime, anywhere from anyone."

—BRAD LEACH

When you were growing up, did you ever have teachers you just didn't gel with? Maybe they were overly hard on you, or perhaps their teaching style didn't mesh with how you liked to learn. Maybe you knew something about them that made them hard to respect. Or it could be that their background was simply different from yours and you found it difficult to relate to them.

Did you learn a lot from those teachers? Probably not.

On the other hand, maybe you remember having a few teachers who really got through to you. (I hope you had teachers like that.) They were easy to respect, and you felt they liked and understood you.

Those were the teachers you wanted to learn from, right?

During our school years, not all teachers were created equal. And that doesn't change as we get older. Learning from some people is easy for us. Learning from others can be difficult. Every day, we make a decision about who we will and who we won't learn from.

But here's the truth both about school and our life today. *Everybody* has something to teach us. If we choose, we can learn from anyone.

But we have to choose.

FINDING YOUR TEACHERS

People with low teachability tend to limit the teachers they allow in their lives. That is, they have determined that there are some people they will learn from and some they won't. People with a different background or worldview, for example, or people with a different religious affiliation or political viewpoint might be deemed off-limits in their mind.

WHEN WE LIMIT WHOM WE WILL LEARN FROM, WE ALSO LIMIT OUR TEACHABILITY.

It's possible you have had a hard time learning from me because I am a pastor and I used church illustrations throughout this book. (That doesn't offend me, by the way. It simply makes my point.) But here's the thing: when we limit whom we will and won't learn from, we also limit our teachability.

This doesn't mean that all voices in our lives are created equal or carry the same weight. That would be simply impossible. But it does mean we owe it to ourselves to actually think about our learning parameters—and expand them whenever we can.

To develop a lifestyle of teachability, I suggest that you give some serious thought to who your chosen teachers are. In fact, I suggest that you proactively identify the following four groups of people or "teachers" and make a conscious determination to learn from them on a consistent basis.

Teacher Strategy #1: Find a Few "Say Anything, Anytime" Teachers.

First of all, you need *a few* people in your life who have been given explicit permission to say anything they want to any area of your life at any time. It's your job to identify these people and do the hard work of developing relationships with them. It's important that these teachers feel comfortable saying potentially hard things to you that no one else can say.

I am not talking about your best friends here, although I suppose it's possible that a close friend could fill this role. I'm basically talking about a small group of intentionally chosen advisors whose opinions and honesty you trust and whose candor you invite.

As a pastor, I have the privilege of being a spiritual influencer in the lives of a lot of people on a weekly basis. Consequently, I understand how much I need others to play this role in my life. So I have selected three to five "overseers"—other pastors that I have asked to be my "say anything, anytime" teachers. Twice a year I schedule a one-hour appointment to bring them up to speed on my life, my priorities, and the major directives of our organization. I send my overseers an agenda in advance and remind them that I want them to speak their minds openly and honestly.

When I recently suggested such an arrangement to a leader I have coached for several years, he said, "For years, I had people who wanted to teach me in this way, but I wouldn't let them." He was beginning to realize that until he was willing to open himself up to a few select voices and give them permission to speak into his life, he would remain at a standstill in regards to reaching his greater potential.

Perhaps you need a few overseers in your life as well. What would it look like to develop strategic relationships with three to five people to whom you give permission to "say anything" on a consistent basis?

Remember, it's your responsibility. If you want to have people in your life who can give you this kind of feedback, then you must take the time to cultivate the relationships. Choose your advisors carefully, be respectful of their time and energy, and make it explicitly clear that they really can say anything to you and you will listen. To develop a lifestyle of teachability, you must do this.

Teacher Strategy #2: Identify Some Distant Mentors.

Being strategic about inviting "say anything" advisors into your life is an important part of establishing a teachable lifestyle. But you can also learn a lot from people you don't even know or know well. I know I would not be who I am today if it weren't for the voices of *distant mentors* in my life.

What is a distant mentor? When you read a book by an expert, you are being influenced by a distant mentor. When you listen to an interview with someone whom you admire, you are being taught by a distant mentor. A distant mentor is someone whom you may never meet or interact with personally, but to whom you have given permission to speak into your life through their books, teachings, podcasts, interviews, lectures, and so forth. They are people whose voices you have come to trust, whom you've chosen to learn from. Never in the history of mankind has it been easier to find people like this who can help shape your life and make you better.

To learn most effectively from your distant mentors, I recommend creating a personal growth plan. This is nothing more than a simple, thought-out strategy of how you intend to grow and learn in the next year.[1] What books are you going to read? What interviews will you listen to? What conferences will you attend? How will you carve out time in your schedule to focus on learning from distant mentors in your life? (I recommend at least one hour per week. Maybe while you are on the treadmill?) If you are intentional about devising your plan and following it, you'll be surprised by the growth you see in your life.

One final thought on distant mentors. In our increasingly connected world, gaining direct access to voices we admire is becoming more and more possible. We might not be able to meet with these people face-to-face, but many choose to be accessible through Twitter, Facebook, or in other small-setting environments they're willing to create. Take advantage of this reality. Find people who have lived your tomorrow[2] and learn from them. It's worth it.

Teacher Strategy #3: Find New Voices and Let Them Stretch You.

When you are defining *teacher* in your life, don't rule out the voices of new thought-leaders in your area of interest. In fact, I recommend that you seek these voices out.

Our world is moving faster and changing more rapidly than at any other time in human history. With all this speed and change comes the emergence of people whose thinking differs markedly from the current norm. If you are going to develop a lifestyle of teachability, then you must keep an open mind toward these new voices, even giving them permission to push the envelope a little bit and be a little bit "out there" from time to time.

Fourteen or fifteen years ago, when we were first beginning Next Level Church, the landscape of how local church was done was changing rapidly. New voices were emerging who used words like *postmodern* and *emergent* and proposed ideas that didn't necessarily fit into the "box" of how most people were doing church.

It was so interesting to watch the established leadership's attitude to what was happening. Some current leaders flat-out rejected these new voices. Others wholeheartedly embraced them. And lots of them, myself included, fell somewhere in between.

During that time, I had several peers ask me what I thought about these "new guys." And my comment was always the same: "I don't agree with everything they are saying. But I think we have to give them permission to stretch the balloon a little bit so that it never quite goes back to the same shape it was before."

That's what new thought-leaders are supposed to do—push the envelope, inflate the balloon. That's how innovation works, and innovation is crucial to keeping people and organizations alive and thriving.

Will we agree with everything these new voices are saying and doing in five years? Probably not. But if I'm honest, when I listen to some of the stuff I taught five years ago, I don't agree with everything I said then either.

Sometimes the best way to stretch yourself is to sit down with a young, less experienced person coming behind you and just listen like crazy. Let their fresh thoughts stretch you, their ideas challenge you. You might not agree with everything they say, but you might not look at the world the same again afterward either.

Teacher Strategy #4: Find a Way for Everybody to Be Your Teacher.

The ultimate goal in developing a lifestyle of teachability is to be able to learn something from everybody. I credit much of the success we had when our organization was in the start-up phase to this principle. We would watch organizations that were ten times our size or organizations that were a hundred times our size. When we saw something we liked, something that seemed to work, we would adapt it for our own purposes.

Even today, we work hard at keeping that "watch and learn" mind-set alive in our organization. And we don't just observe organizations that are larger than we are. We also are watching those who are a tenth of our size. We have determined that everyone can be a teacher to us and that we can all be better because of it.

This principle doesn't just apply to organizations, of course. And it doesn't just have to involve watching and observing. Why not make friends with those who could teach you? Why not ask questions over a cup of coffee or on a comments page on someone's blog? Teachers are everywhere if you look for them and are willing to learn.

If you're a stay-at-home parent, where can you learn more about child rearing, home organization, or making extra money?

Consider other moms at playgroups, classes at your gym, blogs and online magazines, people you knew at school, even members of your own family. And keep in mind that you can learn from others' mistakes as well as their example.

If you're a twentysomething fresh out of college, who can you begin paying attention to who can help you with your transition into the next season of your life? Possibilities are work colleagues, fellow alumni, school officials, even friends of your parents.

For newlyweds who want to get better at being married, learning opportunities abound—classes, workshops, and the advice of friends. And don't forget to observe couples whose relationships you admire.

You get the point. If you want to live a lifestyle of teachability, you will constantly be on the lookout for teachers who help you learn how to become better than you are today. Observe people whose lives seem to work. Compare notes. Ask questions. (We'll explore some tips on doing this in the next chapter.) Learn from your chosen teachers any way you can.

Developing a lifestyle of teachability is not a halfway commitment. As John Maxwell stresses, it's really a matter of developing the kind of "mind-set that teachable people carry with them wherever they go."[3]

The ultimate goal is to see everyone, everywhere, every day as a teacher you can learn from. That's what it means to live a lifestyle of teachability.

NOTES

1. For a long time, when I heard people talk about a "personal growth plan," I was like, "What the heck are you even talking about?" I wanted one, but I thought I didn't know the first thing about what having one

would be like. So finally, after about fifteen years of hearing that, I came up with a nine-minute strategy for how to create a simple personal growth plan for yourself or for any member of your team. You can listen to it free at www.MattKellerOnline.com/developmentplan.

2. I wish this phrase were original to me, but it's not. My friend Micah Pelkey was the first person I ever heard use it. And the minute he did, I knew instantly that I was going to steal it, adopt it, and use it like crazy. Thanks for the phrase, Micah. Here's your credit.

3. John Maxwell, *Sometimes You Win—Sometimes You Learn*, 123.

Chapter 12

Learn the Art of Asking Great Questions

If you want to be successful and reach your leadership
potential, you need to embrace asking questions as a lifestyle.

—JOHN C. MAXWELL

A t the end of the last chapter we said that the ultimate goal of a teachable lifestyle is to see everyone we meet as someone we can learn from. King Solomon from ancient Israel, the son of King David, whom we've referenced earlier in the book, actually spoke to this notion when he wrote,

> *The purpose in a man's heart is like deep water,*
> *but a man of understanding will draw it out.*[1]

Every person we meet is someone with a deep-water heart. Unfortunately, the average person doesn't know how to draw out the wisdom hidden in hearts all around them. But people who develop a lifestyle of teachability learn how to do this by asking great questions.

For years, I have worked hard to teach my two boys, Will and Drew, to think in terms of asking questions. I have taught them to always be ready with a question for the people they meet, whether it's the waiter from another country on our cruise ship or an influential leader they have a chance to meet while in a green room[2] with me prior to a speaking engagement. And I try to model what I teach by asking questions myself. Good questions are tools that draw out the wisdom contained deep inside someone else. You will never reach your full teachable potential without learning to ask them well. The following eleven tips will help you do that.

Question Tip #1: Practice Thinking, "If I Could Spend an Hour with _____, What Would I Ask?"

When you train your mind to think in terms of asking questions, you will begin to see everyone as someone you can learn from. I will often practice this kind of thinking by making a list of a half-dozen questions I would ask someone if I met him or her. For example, if I met a celebrity like Jimmy Fallon or Jim Carrey, what would I want to know? But I don't just do this with famous people. I also practice by thinking about what I would ask a restaurant manager or local business owner. I have found that training my brain this way makes me a better question asker.

Along the same lines, I am convinced that everyone should have an ongoing list of people with whom they would like to spend an hour. Your list won't look like mine, but that's the whole point. Some people on your list should be famous people you are not likely to meet, but others should be people you could conceivably encounter in the next year or two. Still others on your list should be peers who basically do what you do. Just having the list will help you think about questions differently.

Question Tip #2: Keep Your Opinions to a Minimum.

When you have a chance to spend time with and ask questions of someone you want to learn from, remember that you're not there to justify yourself in front of that person. You are there to learn from him or her. And the simple reality is that if you're talking, you're not learning.

Talking too much is one of the biggest mistakes I see people make when they attempt to ask questions. They end up squandering the opportunity to plumb the deep waters of wisdom before them.

It's worth noting that overtalking is often due to nervousness. When we are nervous, we tend to talk longer and speak less succinctly than we normally would. Being conscious of this and preparing questions ahead of time can help you fight this tendency.

Question Tip #3: Frame It Up, Then Shut Up (In Other Words, Ask a Great Lead Question).

Most questions or series of questions will require a certain amount of framing up—giving background and so forth—before the interview can progress. But nerves and excitement can cause us to spend way too long on this framing process and end up eating into the time we could be listening and learning. That's the reason for what I call the "frame it up, then shut up" principle.

When I want someone's advice or perspective on an issue I'm

dealing with, I give myself no more than three minutes to give the necessary background and ask my question. If it turns out that the person I am interviewing needs more information once he or she begins sharing advice, I've found I can politely stop that person and fill in the blanks.

After you've framed up a situation in no more than three minutes, then the greatest question you can lead off with is, "If you were me, what would you do?" This question takes all of the other person's wisdom and life experience and instantly puts it in your shoes. When you ask this question of people, they will tell you how they would deal with your situation from their perspective. It truly is the greatest question you can ask someone else.

> **"IF YOU WERE ME, WHAT WOULD YOU DO?"**

Question Tip #4: Key In on What Really Matters to Both of You.

I have wasted many a precious minute in an interview with someone I wanted to learn from because I let the conversation veer toward a topic neither of us really cared about. If I had stayed focused on where the other person's expertise and interest coincided with areas of relevance for me, I would have benefited more.

Most successful people have opinions on just about everything and will answer whatever you ask. But great questions focus the conversation and key in on their specific area of expertise and passion.

Several years ago, at a leadership event, I watched a well-known national news reporter interview college football great Tim Tebow and his longtime coach at the University of Florida, Urban Meyer. The interview was slated to last thirty minutes.

But the interviewer wasted at least fifteen of those with a series of shallow, surface-level questions about his "polarizing personality." Finally Coach Meyer stopped her. "Listen," he said (or something to that effect). "This is a leadership event, and we have one of the greatest leaders around up here. If I were you, I would be asking Tim questions about how he leads instead of all these other issues that aren't helping anybody."

It was a magnificent, eye-opening moment for the reporter and the entire room. I certainly learned from watching it. I learned that the most productive questions in any interview are those that focus on the expertise and passion of the person being interviewed.

The way to know that you've hit a vein of expertise and passion in those you are questioning is to watch their body language. They will sit up in their chair and look as if they're coming alive. When you hit one of these veins in your conversation, stay in it as long as you possibly can. Keep asking follow-up questions that pertain to the same subject. Trust me, there is pure gold just ahead in your conversation. Some of the greatest insights I have gleaned have come from such "passion runs" that emerged during a conversation or in an interview.

Question Tip #5: Do Your Homework.

Before you meet with people you desire to learn from, spend some time researching them. Find out about their personal background, their work experience, their current reality. Listen to a few of their latest talks. Review their website if they have one. Follow them on Twitter and pay attention to the things they're focused on right now.

I have found that the more preparation I do beforehand, the

better use I can make of my time in an interview. Unfortunately I learned this the hard way.

Several years ago, I had the opportunity to spend an hour with the mayor of our city. It was an appointment I had anticipated for a long time. To say I was excited and nervous was an understatement. When the day finally arrived, we sat down at the conference table in the mayor's office and started our conversation. Everything was going well. I was taking notes, and he was loosening up.

Then I asked him a question about his future vision for our city. To which he replied, "Well, seeing as I've been in office for nine years and my term ends in six weeks, I don't suppose it matters much, does it?"

I felt like an absolute idiot. If I had done my homework, I would have known the mayor was leaving office in six weeks and would not have asked that particular question. He was gracious, of course, but our interview never quite got back on track.

I have reaped massive dividends from that lesson since then. Never do I go into a meeting with anyone without being prepared.

Question Tip #6: Come Up with Way More Questions Than You Need.

An important part of doing your homework before an interview is to prepare the questions you want to be ready to ask. It's important to come up with more questions than you think you need. In fact, if you're spending an hour with someone, I recommend coming up with at least eighty-six questions you can ask.[3]

Why so many, you ask? Surely you won't use all those in an interview. And that's true. But if you only prepare four or five questions you want to ask someone, chances are they won't be the best questions you could ask. But if you force yourself to come up with eighty-six questions, then I promise you, out of the eighty-six questions, you'll find eight or nine great ones! Also, if you prepare eighty-six questions, you'll be ready for unexpected shifts in the conversation. No matter which way the interview goes, you will have pertinent questions.

Question Tip #7: Take Notes—Preferably on Paper.

When you're spending time with people you desire to learn from, show them the respect of taking notes. You'll probably also find that writing down what you hear helps you retain the information better. But if you are going to take notes on a technology device, which in my opinion is not as good as pen and paper,[4] be sure to tell them that's what you're doing, so they don't think you're texting or checking e-mail during the interview. And since we're talking about electronic devices, be sure you put your phone on airplane mode when you meet with someone you desire to learn from. Nothing breaks the flow of thought and conversation like a phone ringing or buzzing on a table. And nothing is ruder than actually answering a call or returning a text when you're with someone you admire and desire to learn from.[5]

Question Tip #8: Always Have a Question Ready.

People who have developed a lifestyle of teachability have learned to always have a question ready at any time and for anyone. They live with the expectation that someone they desire to learn from could cross their path at any given moment.

Several years ago I was speaking at a conference in Orlando when a leader I have admired and learned much from over the years but never actually met stepped into the elevator with me. I stood there dumbfounded for about three seconds, then I realized I had twenty seconds to learn from one of the great leaders of my time.

So what did I do?

Nothing.

I chickened out. I squandered my opportunity to ask this leader a question when I had the chance. Instead of seizing the moment, I let my pride and fear get the best of me.

Do you know how much learning can take place in twenty seconds in an elevator? I guess I'll never know. But I guarantee I'll have a question ready next time.

Question Tip #9: Avoid "Best, Worst, and One" Questions.

Contrary to popular belief and common habit, one of the worst questions you can ask is one that includes the words *best*, *worst*, or *one*. For example,

- What was the best thing about your vacation?
- What is the worst thing about being in your position?
- What one piece of advice would you give a young leader like me?

Here's why these are weak questions. Questions that include these three words send the other person's mind racing, mentally comparing experiences and trying to narrow down what "the one" or "the best" is. Trying to come up with a single answer will put that person in a mental bind from trying to filter out all the other possible responses. But when you're interviewing someone you want to learn from, you don't want that person to waste time trying to come up with a single response. You want that person to talk out loud so you can learn.

A better way to ask the questions above would be,

- What were two or three of the best things about your vacation?
- What are two or three of the worst things about being in your position?
- What two or three pieces of advice would you give a young leader like me?

A person who is asked a "one" question will always have an extended period of silence before he or she answers. But a person asked a "two or three" question will usually begin talking immediately. And from a learning perspective, isn't learning two or three things better than just learning one? You don't *just* want to know one thing, do you?

Question Tip #10: Think of Questions as Camera Angles.
In my opinion, one of the most important advancements of modern sports has been the introduction of instant replay. Every major professional sport now uses instant replay to get the referees' calls right. And referees know that the more camera angles they can get on a play, the better. Every different angle gives them a chance to see and learn something new about what just happened.

What's true in instant replay is also true in our quest to develop a lifestyle of teachability. The more perspectives you can get on an issue or an idea, the better you will understand it. In that vein, I have found it extremely helpful to think of my questions as camera angles on an experience in someone's life. Each question has the potential to provide you with new information that can help you see something you wouldn't have seen before.

I have eight or ten go-to "camera angles" that I use as filters when I'm thinking about the questions I want to ask, but of course there are endless possibilities. The "camera angles" will vary depending on whom you're talking to and what you want to learn in that moment.

For example, when I had the chance to spend fifteen minutes in the locker room with the offensive coordinator for the Baltimore Ravens on a game day, my "camera" immediately focused on different aspects of leadership:

- How do you lead guys you didn't pick but were chosen for you?
- How do you lead guys who make more money than you and are more famous than you?
- How do you lead guys who didn't have father figures growing up?
- How do you handle the pressure of knowing the decisions you make on the field today will be scrutinized by millions of people?
- How does that affect your family?

Did you see how many different "shots" I took in a short amount of time? And because I've made it a habit to think this way, I could easily have kept asking such questions off the top of my head for ninety minutes. Thinking of questions in terms of camera angles is a habit worth developing if you want to be teachable.

Question Tip #11: Go Deep.

Several years ago, Sarah and I had lunch with a couple we were mentoring. After we paid the bill, we ended up drifting around a mall with them for a couple of hours, then stopping for ice cream. We spent the majority of the afternoon together. But when Sarah and I got in the car late that afternoon, we both looked at each other and said, "What happened?"

Now understand, this was not a social get-together. The time had been set aside for mentoring. This was a couple we believed in, saw potential in, and were excited to impart wisdom to. But in all our time together, we had not once talked about anything that really mattered.

For the next several minutes, we dissected why the day had slipped away without this couple taking advantage of the opportunity they had been given to learn. That's when we were reminded of a verse in Proverbs that's very much like the one quoted at the beginning of this chapter:

> *Wise words are like deep waters;*
> *wisdom flows from the wise like a bubbling brook.*[6]

That couple had been sitting next to a deep well all day and just hadn't bothered to dip into it.

Teachable people never miss an opportunity to draw out the water of wisdom from the deep wells they are connected to. They're always ready to dive deeper into the minds and hearts of those they have the opportunity to learn from. And the way they do this is through what I call deep-well questions.

Surface-level questions are what you would expect them to be. Surfacy. Shallow. They're questions like,

- How are you doing?
- How are your children?
- Do you have any vacations planned?

Although these questions invite conversation, they don't necessarily invite teachability because they don't lead the person to dip into the deep well of his or her experience. But a deep-well question is designed to go below the surface.

- What are you learning in your current season of life?
- What have you tried to teach your children in the last six months?
- How do you think about and plan for your vacation time?

See the difference?

"Wise words are like deep waters." Knowing how to ask good questions draws that deep water out. A well-phrased question or angle can take the person you're trying to learn from in unexpected directions.

Now, I sometimes get pushback when I talk about this kind of question. "I don't want to constantly be pestering my friends and others with all these deep-well questions. Won't they get annoyed?" To which I would honestly say no. In my experience, people who have water to give usually enjoy giving it. In fact, they usually feel respected and appreciated when someone acknowledges their wisdom and seeks to draw it out.

> **SOMEONE WHO HAS WATER TO GIVE USUALLY ENJOYS GIVING IT.**

On the rare occasion when someone is tired of talking or

THE KEY TO EVERYTHING

isn't in a mood to share a whole lot, trust me, you'll be able to pick up those cues easily. Most deep-well people are emotionally aware enough to let you know they've had enough of your questions. It can be something as subtle as "I don't know, man . . ." or, "That's kind of a heavy question over ice cream." In which case, you simply take the hint and move back up to something more surface level. Trust me, you'll know when that is, and it won't be as often as you think.

What Great Questions Can Do

Solomon said that the heart of a man is a deep well and that only a person of insight can draw it out. That's what great questions can do for you—help you draw out hidden wisdom. You can learn something from everybody, but only if you know the right questions and how to ask them.

> YOU CAN LEARN SOMETHING FROM EVERYBODY, BUT ONLY IF YOU KNOW THE RIGHT QUESTIONS TO ASK.

The great genius Albert Einstein said it a different way: "It is not that I'm so smart. But I stay with the questions much longer."[7] Developing a lifestyle of teachability demands that you learn to stay with the questions longer.

Try it. I think you'll like the payoff.

NOTES

1. Proverbs 20:5 esv.

2. Why are green rooms never green? (At least they aren't in my

experience.) Someday I'm going to find one. If you have one, I want to see it.

3. People ask me all the time when I teach this principle, "Why eighty-six questions?" To which I always reply, "I don't know. Because it's less than one hundred, which sounds like a *lot* and might make you shut down, but it's way more than twelve, so it helps you realize how important it is to stretch yourself."

4. Recent studies have supported what I have found from my experience. First, taking notes with pen and paper does help us remember key facts better than simply remembering what we heard. (See Dustin Wax, "Writing and Remembering: Why We Remember What We Write," Lifehack.org, http://www.lifehack.org/articles/productivity/writing-and-remembering-why-we-remember-what-we-write.html, accessed January 2015.) And second, we actually take more effective notes by hand than we do with a laptop or other electronic device. (See Robinson Meyer, "To Remember a Lecture Better, Take Notes by Hand," *Atlantic,* May 1, 2014, http://www.theatlantic.com/technology/archive/2014/05/to-remember-a-lecture-better-take-notes-by-hand/361478/.)

5. If something is so urgent that you *have* to take a call, you're probably not ready to be sitting in this meeting. And if you just "have to return a text real quick," you probably think you're more important than you are.

6. Proverbs 18:4 NLT.

7. I suppose I should say that Albert Einstein is supposed to have said this. This is one of those quotes that is all over the Internet but with no real proof that Einstein actually said it. That's all right with me. The point is a good one regardless of whether or not Einstein actually said it.

Chapter 13

Get Wisdom

Knowledge speaks, but wisdom listens.

—JIMI HENDRIX[1]

Teachability has the power to get you a lot of things in life. It can get you wealth. It can get you a promotion. It can get you better communication between you and your spouse. It can get you inroads into places you could never go otherwise. But there is something that teachability can get you that trumps all those other things. The most important and powerful thing teachability can get you is wisdom.

Now I know that at this point you may be thinking something like what you thought at the beginning of the book, *Seriously Matt, wisdom? That's the most important thing I can get?*

Yes, seriously. Don't miss this one. It's one of the most important concepts in the entire book.

King Solomon, whom we referenced in the last chapter, made an interesting comment when he wrote,

The beginning of wisdom is this: Get wisdom.
Though it cost all you have, get understanding.[2]

Did you see it? Wisdom *is* the most important thing we can get! If there is one thing that trumps all when it comes to a lifestyle of teachability, it is the principle of getting wisdom.

TEACHABILITY AND WISDOM

Teachability and wisdom are next-door neighbors, identical twins, two sides of the same coin. In fact, you could say that teachability is simply wisdom in attitude form.

I believe the pursuit of wisdom is one of the most underrated quests in the world today. Though people seek out principles and knowledge and chase after other ideals and ideas like crazy, very few books or teachings actually focus on wisdom.

Yet wisdom is the secret weapon of success in your life. There is no decision you will ever make that won't benefit from having it. And the opposite is also true. Every decision suffers when it's made without wisdom.

> IF THERE IS ONE THING THAT TRUMPS ALL THE OTHERS WHEN IT COMES TO A LIFESTYLE OF TEACHABILITY, IT IS THE PRINCIPLE OF GETTING WISDOM.

THE BEST QUESTION EVER

Pastor and author Andy Stanley wrote a great book a decade ago called *The Best Question Ever*.[3] Its premise was that the best question anyone can ever ask when making a decision is, "What is the wise thing to do?"

Not, "What is the smart thing or the right thing?"

Not, "What is the legal thing?"

Not even, "What is the moral thing to do?"

All those questions are important, of course. But according to Andy, the wisdom question trumps them all. That's because asking "What is the wise thing to do?" provides an instant filter for making the best decision possible in any given situation.

> **THE BEST QUESTION ANYONE CAN EVER ASK WHEN MAKING A DECISION IS, "WHAT IS THE WISE THING TO DO?"**

Andy goes on to suggest adding three clarifying elements to the question that help define what wisdom looks like even in complex situations. He says to ask the question in three different ways—in light of past experience, present circumstances, and future hopes and dreams. Framing a decision inside our past experiences gives it personal potency. Framing it inside our present circumstances gives it immediate application. And framing a decision in the context of our future hopes and dreams helps us take the long view, considering eventual outcomes as well as present needs.

Andy contends that when we ask the wisdom question and use those three filters, our decision making will instantly improve. Ever since my wife and I got turned on to this question, our decision making has completely changed. It truly is the best question ever.

That's the power of wisdom.

Wisdom at our Fingertips

When I was eighteen years old, I attended a summer camp where I learned something that changed my life. As we sat on our beds in a second-story dorm room one night, our camp counselor shared a challenge with us that I have never forgotten. In fact it has shaped me into who I am today. Sarah and I credit much of our success throughout our life to this one strategy my camp counselor taught me more than twenty years ago.[4]

On that hot summer night in 1993, my camp counselor encouraged a dorm full of us boys to adopt a practice of reading one chapter every day from a book in the Bible called Proverbs. He told us the book of Proverbs was a "book of wisdom" consisting of thirty-one short chapters. Because there are thirty-one days in most months, it's easy to read a different chapter every day and the entire book every month.

"If you'll start doing this," he told us, "you'll have the wisdom you need to become as successful as you desire to be."[5]

When I returned home from camp that summer, I decided to take my counselor's advice. I began a daily practice of reading the chapter of Proverbs that lined up with the date on the calendar. And sure enough, over the next several years of my life, my life started changing. I began making better decisions. I became more teachable and more successful. At the age of twenty-three, I even became a national youth director for the organization I was then part of.

The book of Proverbs is one of the easiest to understand and most potent wisdom reservoirs anywhere. There are 924 verses or "sayings" in the book, and 282 of them speak directly to the idea of "wisdom," "being wise," "receiving instruction," and "gaining understanding." That's a 30 percent potency level right there! And the other 600 or so verses are powerful as well.

There are so many nuggets of wisdom hidden inside the book of Proverbs that I have made it my personal life mission to mine them all out before I die. And trust me, it's going to take me my whole life to do it. I've been doing it since I was eighteen, and I'm still finding fresh wisdom in that book every day.

Just to give you a taste of what I'm talking about, here are a few verses that pertain to wisdom, and then my personal translation underneath.

The one who gets wisdom loves life;
the one who cherishes understanding will soon prosper.

My translation: If you love your life and want to prosper, get wisdom.

Fools find no pleasure in understanding
but delight in airing their own opinions.

My translation: Sometimes you need to shut your mouth to keep people from knowing how foolish you really are.

Wisdom yields patience.

My translation: Not everything good in life happens all at once. Sometimes you've got to wait for some of the best stuff. Relax, calm down, and let the ball come to you.

> *Listen to advice and accept discipline,*
> *and at the end you will be counted among the wise.*

My translation: If you'll quit acting like you know it all—if you'll humble yourself and listen to others who are farther along than you—one day people will look up and call you awesome.[6]

Even though I have read the book of Proverbs several dozen times in my life now, it never ceases to amaze me how I can find new things every time I read it. I credit so much of the success I have experienced in my life to this one simple principle of getting wisdom on a regular basis.

I DARE YOU

So here's my challenge to you. I dare you to start reading a chapter of Proverbs a day. The average chapter has about twenty-five verses in it, some more, some less, so it shouldn't take you more than five minutes to read. Then pick one verse that jumps out at you and write it down.

Don't worry. Even if you don't read every day, what you do read will still have an effect on your life. Think about it. Even if you read a chapter only three times per week, in a year's time you would still have read about 3,750 sayings and nuggets on wisdom.

Do you think your decision-making and your thinking would be better or worse for having read 3,750 phrases about wisdom and written more than 150 of them down? That's a no-brainer. Your life can't help but be better with that kind of wisdom dripping in on a consistent basis.

So will you do it? There's nothing stopping you except for a simple decision to start getting wisdom in your life on a regular basis. You will never regret it.

Gaining access to the book of Proverbs has never been easier, by the way. It is as easy as stepping into a bookstore, ordering an e-book, or downloading a free Bible app on your smartphone. You'll find there are a number of translations available. I recommend either *The Message* or the New International Version, also known as the NIV. Either of these are very easy to read and understand. So now the next time you are sitting on an airplane or waiting in line at the doctor's office, you can be growing your teachability by gaining wisdom.

FINAL THOUGHTS ON WISDOM

In life there are a whole lot of things you can strive to get, but only one will position you for everything else: wisdom. The path to developing a lifestyle of teachability is paved with wisdom.

Take the dare.

Get wisdom.

You'll be so glad you did.

NOTES

1. If you would have bet me twenty dollars when I first started writing this book that I would be including a quote by Jimi Hendrix, I would have lost that bet, because I just did. And it's in the wisdom chapter, of all places.

2. Solomon wrote this in Proverbs 4:7.

3. Andy Stanley's book is called *The Best Question Ever: A Revolutionary Approach to Decision Making* (Colorado Springs: Multnomah, 2004).

4. By the way, my camp counselor had the sweetest mullet hairstyle ever. Hey, it was cool back then.

5. I also remember that counselor saying that "Wisdom is the key to everything." Hmm. Now where have I heard that phrase recently?

6. The proverbs quoted here are 19:8, 18:2, 19:11, and 19:20, all NIV except my own translations.

Chapter 14

Know Yourself Well

Know yourself. Don't accept your dog's admiration
as conclusive evidence that you are wonderful.

—ANN LANDERS

A few years ago I had the opportunity to spend a couple of
hours with Rick Warren.

Rick is the founder and senior pastor of one of the largest
churches in the United States, Saddleback Church in Southern
California. His book *The Purpose Driven Life*[1] is considered the
bestselling hardcover nonfiction book in history besides the
Bible, and Rick is consistently ranked as one of the most influential leaders in the world.[2] He also is a brilliant thinker who
literally has an idea a minute and is more than happy to share
them, which for an idea guy like me is a lot of fun.

However, the thing that struck me the most about being with
Rick Warren when I met him was how confident and secure he is.
He seems to have a clear handle on who he is, what his presence

means, and how he can and should leverage that to bring joy to people and benefit to life-giving causes. There's nothing arrogant about him, but he doesn't carry himself like, "Aw, shucks, I just got lucky," either. He is extremely aware of what has been entrusted to him, the responsibility that comes with it, and how he is accountable to use it for good. He understands who he is and is comfortable with that.

At one point during our time together, we were walking through a giant outdoor courtyard. As various people walked up and said hello to Rick, he would stop and ask, "Would you like a picture?" with the biggest smile on his face. Then he would hand their smartphones to me, and I would become the makeshift photographer for their moment with Rick Warren.

Why would he do that? It certainly wasn't because he needed to have one more picture taken of himself. He did that because he understood who he was and what people most wanted from a chance interaction with *the* Rick Warren!

It was this two-hour interaction with Rick that led to his writing the foreword to my book, *God of the Underdogs*.[3] Rick understood what his stamp of approval on my work would do for me, and he graciously agreed to do it—yet another example of his self-awareness.

Rick Warren's level of self-awareness is a model for all of us. He truly personifies what it means to walk confidently in who he is privileged to be.

BEGINNING OUR DESCENT

We are now officially just two chapters away from finishing this book. Your to-do-list-checking side is probably going crazy right now, and you're thinking, *Come on, man. I just gotta finish this thing!* Or maybe you're surprised that you made it this far. You may even be thinking, *Thank God this is almost over.*

Listen, no matter what your reaction, let me just say congratulations—and thanks for sticking with me.[4]

In this second-to-last chapter of the book, we are going to explore why knowing yourself is so important to developing a lifestyle of teachability. After all, you are the only person you will spend your entire life with, so the more self-aware you are, the more teachable you can become, and the more possible it will be to reach your full potential.

Why is self-awareness so important to teachability? Simply this: people who don't know and understand themselves don't see their behaviors accurately in the mirror and therefore can't make course corrections when they are needed. To develop a lifestyle of teachability, you must be self-aware in the following four areas.

Self-Awareness Tip #1: Be Aware of Your Strengths.

Self-aware people know their strengths. The best definition of a strength I have ever heard comes from business author and researcher Marcus Buckingham,[5] who essentially says that a strength is not "something you're good at," but rather "any activity that makes you feel strong." According to that definition, nobody else can tell you what your strengths are. Only you can figure out what makes you feel strong.

Teachable people—people who are committed to growing and reaching their full potential—organize their lives and work to take full advantage of their strengths. For example, writing and speaking is a strength for me—not because I'm good at it, although I appreciate it if someone says so, but because after I have written something significant or spoken in front of a group of people, I feel like I am the king of the world. Writing and speaking make me feel strong.

Conversely, I am pretty good at returning e-mails and clearing out my inbox. After I've done that, however, I don't feel like a million bucks. Instead, I feel like I want to pull my hair out.

Writing and speaking is a strength for me, then. Handling e-mails is not.

What are your strengths? Do you know them? Knowing your strengths will help you develop a lifestyle of teachability because you ultimately add the most value to the world in the area of your strengths. Once you know where you add the most value to the world, you can begin to focus your learning and development.

Knowing who you are gives you the opportunity to know the areas to which you should be devoting more time and energy and also the areas where you should be spending less time and energy. In areas that make you feel strong, lean in and focus more of your time and energy there. In areas that are weaknesses to you, don't spend a ton of time trying to prop those up and get better at them. Focused teachability in your areas of strength will multiply the value you add to the

> **A PERSON WITH GREAT STRENGTHS AND WEAK CHARACTER IS DANGEROUS.**

world around you and focused neglect in your areas of weakness will pay dividends as well.

Now when I say weaknesses, I am of course not talking about character weaknesses. Those fall into their own category and must be dealt with aggressively. After all, a person with great strengths and weak character is dangerous.

Remember King Saul? You must deal with your character issues. That is paramount to your success as well.

Self-Awareness Tip #2: Pay Attention to Your Tendencies.

People with a high level of teachability know their tendencies and know how to navigate with and through them to be successful in life.

What are tendencies? They're simply the basics of your temperament and your general attitude. They're the way you tend to think and react—the way you tend to lean in to certain circumstances. They're not set in stone; you can always choose to respond differently. But they are intrinsic to you, and being aware of them can make you more teachable.

For instance, one of the most important tendencies to be aware of is your general outlook on life. Each of us has a certain way of seeing and responding to the world—a worldview. Some people have a more pessimistic outlook, for instance, while others tend to be more optimistic. Knowing your tendency in your outlook will help you in developing a lifestyle of teachability because you'll know where you're starting from.

For example, I tend to be an optimist by nature. I see the glass as half full most of the time. As the leader of a sizeable organization, this is a good thing . . . most of the time.

Additionally, I have a tendency to be quite persuasive. This, too, can be a good thing . . . most of the time. Put them together and you could say my general outlook is to be a persuasive optimist.

There are times, however, when my persuasive optimism can cause my team to get overwhelmed by my enthusiasm and can create an atmosphere where they hesitate to bring up certain essential pieces of information that might be considered bad news. In other words, they're afraid to rain on my parade.

Knowing this tendency has taught me over the years to urge my team to tell me what I am not seeing. This is not an easy thing for me to do. After all, I don't want to be dragged down by the details of what could go wrong or by the potential holes in a plan. I would rather focus on the positives and the possibilities, fueling myself with visions of how successful something can be. But this is precisely why I need to be teachable with my team around me. They give me eyes to see what I would otherwise have a tendency to look past or ignore.

What is your tendency when it comes to your general outlook on life? How does it affect the people you work with? What about at home with your spouse or kids? Being aware of your basic outlook on life increases your teachability and increases the chances of your success.

A second tendency you must be aware of is your reaction to correction and criticism. Let me use myself as the illustration again. I'm the kind of person who thrives on affirmation. I tend to want everybody to like me, and in the past, I have reacted strongly to any kind of correction or criticism.

In the early years of my leadership journey, this tendency could be a problem. One nasty e-mail would put me down for the count. But becoming aware of this tendency has allowed me to take a more balanced approach to the correction and criticism that come my way. I have learned to ask myself if the people dishing out criticism have my best interest at heart or if they're simply vomiting up their own unhealthiness on me. If it's the former, I know I should listen. If the latter, I can simply dismiss it or figure out a more useful response.

What is your tendency when it comes to criticism? Do you clam up? Shut down? Get defensive? Write off your critics? Knowing your tendency in this area can really enhance your teachability.

A third area where you need to know your tendency involves how you handle positive feedback and praise. Some people tend to let praise and compliments go to their heads and puff up their egos. Others do the exact opposite and never allow any good word to sink in. I think the healthiest approach lies somewhere between the two extremes, where we don't think more highly of ourselves than we ought to, but we also don't think less of ourselves than is accurate.

Knowing your tendency in this area is helpful because how you handle praise has a direct effect on how teachable you will be when you receive a compliment. What's your tendency when praise comes your way? Do you let it go to your head? Do you let it touch your heart? Do you brush it off and dismiss it? Knowing your tendency in this area directly affects your teachability.

These three are only a few possible tendencies we need to be aware of in our lives. There are plenty of others. Some people have a tendency to make excuses or to blame others when problems arise. Some people always feel compelled to spell out every negative possibility, while others, like myself, tend to be overly optimistic in the face of grim circumstances.

It's important to keep in mind that tendencies are not bad or good in and of themselves. They are simply tendencies, personal quirks, and leanings. But paying attention to your tendencies and adjusting accordingly can help you a lot in developing a lifestyle of teachability.

Self-Awareness Tip #3: Pay Attention to Your Rhythms.

I love music. When my brother and I were young, my mom gave us piano lessons, and I spent much of my childhood and teen years singing in choirs and performing on stages doing musical theater and drama.[6]

Growing up musical taught me the power of rhythm, which is the backbone to any piece of music. If the rhythm is unsteady and unpredictable, the song will be a mess. However, if the rhythm is consistent, the music has the potential to be great.

The same is true in our lives as well. Knowing yourself means knowing your personal rhythms. It means understanding how your life flows best, where the highs and lows are, and how to maximize the rises and minimize the falls that are inevitably present in our lives.

For example, I am a morning person and have learned to organize my day around my personal rhythm, with a heavy leaning toward the morning. I do much of my creative writing in the morning. Because I want my team to have me at my best and not get the leftovers, I tend to schedule meetings for the early part of my day.[7] My creativity tends to wane as the day wears on, and by late evening my fuse tends to be shorter than I want it to be. By recognizing these rhythms and planning accordingly, I have learned I can avoid a lot of frustration and misunderstandings.

What about you? What is the best rhythm for your day? When are you at your best—or low on energy? Knowing this will help you up your teachability in your daily routine.

Not only does a day have rhythm, but so do weeks and months as well. My wife and I are very deliberate about the rhythm of our calendar over the course of a year. We know when our life is travel heavy and when it slows down. We know when the church we lead will need our attention the most and when we can be more disconnected.

What about you? When was the last time you stopped to examine the rhythm of your calendar? You might be amazed at what you discover when you do.

Teachable people are not just aware of their own rhythms but keep in mind the rhythms of those around them as well. As a parent, I have had to become aware of the rhythms of my two boys. I may be a morning person, but that doesn't mean they are. At times in my life I have had to adjust my rhythms to theirs in order to be a more effective dad.

If you're an employee, you need to be aware of the rhythms of your boss. Success and failure in your job could very well hinge upon understanding how and when to communicate your ideas upward. Is it possible you're not as successful as you could be simply because you've not been as aware as you need to be of your boss's rhythms?

Spouses, do you know the rhythms of your husband or wife? When is she at the peak of her energy? When is he drained and in need of special consideration? When is the best time for the two of you to connect?

Students, do you know the rhythm of your teachers? Teachers, do you know the rhythm of your students?

Rhythm matters. Keeping it in mind as you organize and plan your life can help you in maximizing teachability in your life.

Self-Awareness Tip #4: Know Your Preferences.

One final concept that matters in terms of knowing yourself is that of learning preferences. Not everyone learns and digests information the same way. You are not like the people in your office or your house, and they are not like you. And you don't have to be.

Knowing your preferences is paramount to increasing your teachability. How do you learn most effectively? Considering some of the following questions for yourself, your children, your employees, or your audience can help make learning easier and more efficient.

- Do you like to read, or do you process ideas better some other way?
- Do e-readers work for you, or do you respond better when you actually hold the paper object in your hands?
- Do you tend to be more visual or more auditory—or are you a hands-on learner?
- Would you rather have someone teach you a skill in person or watch a YouTube video?
- Does physical activity (such as listening to talks while exercising) help you process information, or do you concentrate better while sitting still?
- When you meet with someone, are you better taking notes on paper or on some kind of device?

Preferences can be adapted and changed, by the way. Just because you've never done something a certain way doesn't mean you can't try it. And even if information isn't presented to you in the form you prefer, you can still learn if you choose to.

I often hear people make excuses for why they can't learn or grow in some area of their lives. Most of the time their excuses are just that—excuses. Sure, there are certain things that will come easier to you and others that won't. But my experience has been that when people have enough desire to learn and willingness to change (remember those two components of teachability?), they will take advantage of any opportunity to learn and grow.

WHAT'S RIGHT FOR YOU

In order to develop a lifestyle of teachability, it is essential to know yourself well. Self-awareness can improve your relationships and enhance communication. It can help you be more proactive and responsive instead of just reactive. Most important, self-awareness increases your ability to be teachable over the long haul. Understanding and accepting your strengths, your tendencies, your rhythms, and your learning style is a critical piece to the teachability puzzle.

NOTES

1. Rick Warren, *The Purpose Driven Life: What on Earth Am I Here For?*, expanded edition (Grand Rapids, MI: Zondervan, 2012).
2. Rick Warren was on the cover of *Time* magazine on August 18, 2008. See http://ti.me/1myhz8E.
3. Matt Keller, *God of the Underdogs: When the Odds Are Against You, God Is For You* (Nashville, TN: Thomas Nelson, 2013).
4. I'm even giving you a prize for making it this far. Seriously, here is a nonpublic link to two talks I've given at two leadership gathering events on this subject of teachability: http://bit.ly/youwinaprizebaby. Enjoy!
5. I highly recommend Marcus's DVD curriculum, *Trombone Player Wanted*, available at https://www.tmbc.com/store/trombone-player-wanted. His in-depth content on strengths and weaknesses will make you better, period. He's brilliant, and he has an amazing British accent.
6. I made my stage debut in 1987 at the age of eleven—playing the little

boy Winthrop in *The Music Man.* Eight years later, I had the good
fortune of playing the lead role of Harold Hill in the same musical. To
this day, it is one of my favorites.

7. Those who have had meetings with me in the four-thirty or five-thirty
   afternoon time slots are starting to realize why I always have that glazed-
   over look on my face.

Chapter 15

Choose to Trade Your Life for Learning

Learning never exhausts the mind.

—LEONARDO DA VINCI

When I was growing up, my buddy Adam and I loved to collect and trade baseball cards.[1] One year we spent the entire summer saving up money from mowing lawns and allowances, then rode our bikes into town on an early morning in August to buy an entire box of cards at the corner store. I still remember the exhilaration of getting back to Adam's house, running up the stairs, locking the door, and opening thirty-six "wax packs" of Topps baseball cards.[2]

After we had opened all thirty-six packs of cards, the fun really began. We spent the next two hours making deals and trading cards back and forth. Unfortunately for me, Adam was a much better negotiator than I was, so he always ended up with all the best cards. At least that's the way I remember it. To this day, my childhood is marked by those afternoons we spent trading baseball cards with each other.

What's true of kids and baseball cards is also true of our lives. Each and every day we trade our lives for something. For some people it's stuff—material possessions. They work and work to see how much they can acquire. They define themselves by what they buy and own—the cars they drive, the houses they live in, the designer clothes they wear. Material wealth clearly matters most to them because they are trading their lives for it.

Other people trade their lives for financial security. They want to know that their nest eggs are secure. They spend next to nothing because they are obsessed with making sure they will be all right if something catastrophic happens.

Still others—women especially—trade their lives for relationship security. They will give up almost anything—even their personal safety—to avoid being alone.

Some people trade their lives for fame and prestige. Their highest aim in life is being known and admired by as many people as possible.

On a more positive note, some people trade their lives for spiritual growth or connection. They are willing to sacrifice personal comfort and security for the sense that they are drawing closer to God.

And then there are the power hungry. They spend their days making sure that they are the one in charge, calling the shots, making things happen, never even noticing they have traded their lives away.

There are a million things we can trade our life for in this world. But in this final chapter of the book, I want to challenge you to trade your life for learning.

Why? Because when you trade your life for learning, all that other stuff takes care of itself. Whatever matters most to you—money, power, good relationships, spiritual satisfaction—are in your grasp if you focus on remaining teachable.

Trading Means Making Choices

One thing I remember from my baseball card days is that the essence of trading is making choices. If my buddy had a Mike Schmidt card that I really wanted, then I would have to give up three rookie cards to get it. If he wanted my Pete Rose card, then he was going to have to pay dearly for it.

Trading always involves choices, and this life offers infinite choices. But for the sake of this book, let me narrow your focus down to three choices that will position you for lifelong teachability. I believe these three choices, when made and managed consistently, will position you for the life you have always dreamed of living.

Choice #1: Choose Not to Be Ignorant.

There is a famous saying that "ignorance is bliss," but that's definitely untrue when it comes to teachability. The opposite is actually true. Ignorance is painful and costly, and the consequences of taking an ignorant approach are harmful in so many ways to our life.

Some people, no matter how much you try to warn them, just won't listen. Ignorant people make a conscious decision

each day *not* to see. They choose to be
ignorant.

The teenager who ignores wise
counsel from teachers or parents, the
worker who refuses to comply with
standard operating procedures because
he "doesn't want to conform," the boss
who will not listen to his team when

> **IGNORANT PEOPLE MAKE A CONSCIOUS DECISION EACH DAY NOT TO SEE.**

they are desperately trying to help him see a problem—all these
are examples of people who have chosen to be ignorant and will
pay a high price for it.

Solomon wrote in the book of Proverbs that

A sensible person sees danger and takes cover,
but the inexperienced keep going and are punished.[3]

When we refuse to listen to wise counsel around us and just
"keep going" as Solomon says, we are headed for trouble. We
must make the decision to be teachable, not ignorant.

Choice #2: Choose Not to Be Indifferent.

Indifferent people do not deliberately choose ignorance,
but they don't go out of their way to seek out learning opportunities either. The vast majority of people in our world today
fall into this category as their default daily choice. They believe
that being neutral toward learning is acceptable. But a car in
neutral can't go anywhere—at least not anywhere fast. People
with an indifferent approach don't see the power that teachability could bring them. Consequently, they never reach their
full potential.

THE KEY TO EVERYTHING

We're talking about the office worker who shows up every day and simply does the minimum. This person has enough skills to survive, but shows no signs of a desire to get better.

We're talking about the boyfriend who can't be bothered to learn more about who his girlfriend is so he can serve and love her better. He just likes having someone to date.

We're talking about the teacher who thinks she's seen it all and is just marking time to retirement—or the student who never misses a day but never cracks a book either.

The danger of indifferent teachability is summed up well in this proverb:

Stop listening to instruction, my son,
and you will stray from the words of knowledge.[4]

In other words, when we don't make a disciplined, deliberate effort to stay engaged, we will tend to drift off in ways that will cost us in the long run. Being indifferent to teachability won't cut it if we are going to become everything we have the potential to become. After all, nobody ever casually drifted up to the doorstep of their dream life.

NOBODY EVER CASUALLY DRIFTED UP TO THE DOORSTEP OF THEIR DREAM LIFE.

Being indifferent to teachability means we have to be forced to learn. In other words, we learn because someone else—a boss, a teacher, a parent, or a spouse—demands it. A husband refuses to change until his wife threatens to leave him. The employee is told she'll be fired if she comes in fifteen minutes late one more time. A looming deadline on Monday morning forces a team member to finally research the presentation. The man learns he may die of a heart attack if he doesn't watch what he eats.

All these are classic examples of people who have to be forced into teachability in their lives. Even our public schools are built on this type of forced teachability.

Now don't get me wrong. I myself am a product of our public schools. My mother taught in them for twenty-five years. Tens of millions of Americans have learned profound and life-altering things during their years in the public schools. But the problem, in my view, is that we have created an entire system that subliminally undercuts the teachable lifestyle.

After all, for thirteen years, children are taught that when something is really important for them to know, an authority figure will make sure they know it. We must be aware of what can happen to students who live with this attitude toward learning for a decade or more. The danger is that they will emerge from their school years somehow believing that they can get by with an indifferent approach to teachability and still achieve their dreams. I don't have to tell you how far off base that thinking is.[5]

Choice #3: Choose Intentional Teachability.

When you make the choice to invite teachability into your life on a daily basis, life becomes an adventure. Every day you are given another opportunity to gather valuable insight that will make you a better person in some way. But you have to take advantage of that opportunity. You have to choose teachability, to be intentional about it.

Intentional teachability means getting to the place where you live by the motto, "I seek out learning every day, because I want to become the best me that I can possibly be." It means actively and strategically seeking out wisdom and insight in every arena of your life—relational, career, health, financial, everything. It means placing yourself in a position where you can learn from people who are farther along the journey than you are, as well as those who are right behind you.

Intentional teachability makes life a party with a thousand gifts to be opened every day. Each new insight, once opened, gives you a greater perspective on who you are, who you were created to be, and how you can be the best you possible.

Proverbs 19:20 projects what living in this category can mean:

Listen to advice and accept discipline,
and at the end you will be counted among the wise.[6]

When we make a lifestyle out of listening to advice, accepting instruction, and seeking out learning wherever we may find it, the end result is that we become wise. We don't just make wise choices or have wisdom. We actually become wise. In other words, we personify wisdom.

Did you ever know anyone like that, someone who always seemed to know the best way to go at every turn? That person didn't get that way by accident. That person became that way by being intentional about his or her teachability.

I want to become that kind of person, and I know you do too. Making the decision to intentionally seek out learning on a daily basis is one of the most dependable paths to teachability.

To learn something from everybody we meet, that's the ultimate goal of teachability. And teachability truly is the key to everything.

NOTES

1. Truth is, I still collect baseball cards. I say I buy them "for my kids." But I buy extra packs for myself, too, and then my boys and I trade them with each other. Every once in a while we'll find out a card is worth a lot of money and try to sell it on eBay. We haven't actually sold one yet, but we talk a big game. And who knows? Maybe it will happen.

2. I don't know why we locked the door to my buddy's room. I guess we were afraid his mom would barge in and steal our cards. By the way, do you remember the gum you used to get inside a pack of cards? I could usually get about eight sticks in my mouth before I started to gag a little. Such great memories from my childhood.

3. You'll find this verse in Proverbs 22:3 HCSB.

4. This is Proverbs 19:27.

5. If you are a teacher, thank you for all you are doing for the next generation. We are *all* in your debt.

6. This version of Proverbs 19:20 is from the New International Version.

Final Thoughts on Teachability

The world we live in has changed. Success no longer comes to the one who works the hardest or tries the most. Success no longer hinges on who you know, what you do, or where you come from. The key to success in the world today is predicated on one single component above all the others, and that is teachability.

It's not something our world talks a lot about. It's not a word that makes it into the mission statements of many companies. Nobody that I know of uses the word in their wedding vows, and it doesn't make it into a lot of graduation speeches. But *teachability*, as you have seen, is a word that affects every arena of your life.

Teachability is a choice.
  Teachability is possible.
    And teachability is essential to getting where you most want to go in life.

WHEN TEACHABILITY IS AT THE CORE OF YOUR LIFE, THE SKY IS THE LIMIT ON WHAT YOU CAN ACHIEVE AND BECOME.

Your success depends on it, and your future resides within it.

Teachability is the only path to the life you dream of living.

When teachability is at the core of your life, the sky is the limit on what you can achieve and become.

It truly is your *Key to Everything*.

Thank-You Notes

(My Homage to Jimmy Fallon)

With a tip of the cap to Jimmy Fallon, the *Tonight Show* host who singlehandedly changed the face of late-night television for a new generation, I decided to do the acknowledgments section of this book a little differently. Jimmy Fallon does his "thank-you notes" each Friday night on the show. If you've never seen him do the routine, you can tune in on Friday or Google a clip—then sit back, laugh, and enjoy. The list you're about to read will be a whole lot funnier when you hear his voice in your head.

So without further ado, here are my *Key to Everything* thank-you notes. (Cue "thank you" music from *Tonight*, which is available for download on www.nbc.com, by the way.)

Thank you, Sarah Keller, for being my wife and standing beside me through yet another grueling writing season. And thank you for moving into the driver's seat once again so the message of this book could get into the hands of as many people as it possibly can.

Thank you, kids' ministry department of our church, for giving up one of your brightly colored rooms for so many days. Hopefully my writing does the loud colors justice.

Thank you, rainy season in Florida, for the dark clouds every afternoon while I was writing. You provided just the right atmosphere for me to take a quick twenty-minute nap most days. I think some of my most creative thoughts after I wake up from one of those.

Thank you, Blythe Daniel, for being a literary agent who gets the job done. Thank you for believing in my voice long before a lot of other people did.

Thank you, Starbucks Frappuccinos in the glass bottle. Even though you're not all icy and whippy like the real Frappuccinos I get at the actual store, you still did your job and kept me caffeinated throughout the writing process.

Thank you, Hyatt Regency, for letting me sit in your lobby for eight hours at a time for several days while I wrote parts of this book. I did use the restroom occasionally, but I didn't flush or wash my hands because I didn't want to steal the water. (Just kidding.)

Thank you, fun-size Twix bars. You were the perfect pick-me-up when I needed picking up in the afternoons.

Thank you, Will and Drew. You guys make being your dad a whole lot of fun. I love that you get my humor, and you keep me humble.

Thank you, Mom and Dad, for being my biggest fans. Your support through the years has made such a difference in what I actually believed I could accomplish.

Thank you, Evernote app. I truly believe you are the single greatest productivity tool ever created.

Thank you, Jack Bauer, for coming back on the air and for providing the greatest cliffhangers of all time.

Thank you, Next Level Church, for being a place that people love, so they can experience a loving God. It's working.

Thank you, leaders everywhere, who got the vision of this book and worked your tails off to get it into the hands of thousands of people.

Thank you, parking blocks, for letting me know when it's time to stop my car when I get in your space. Seriously, I couldn't park my car without you.

Thank you, Sunday Night Baseball on ESPN, for *never* coming to Tampa Bay to do a game. I know our stadium is awful, but the baseball is still pretty good.

Thank you, Do Not Disturb Feature on the iPhone, for being the best invention ever. Now I can go to sleep knowing that all my text messages will be silently, patiently waiting for me when I wake up.

Thank you, people who mow my yard, and whom I don't pay because your fee is included in my monthly homeowners' association dues. You really don't understand what a blessing you are to me, especially in the summer when it's something like 190,000 degrees in Florida.

Thank you, my assistant, Cheri, if people really knew how you keep me headed in the right direction, they'd be amazed. Don't worry. I'm not telling.

Thank you, Mike Ash, for taking the whole journey with me. Who'd'a thought, my friend? Who'd'a thought? Well I guess we did, didn't we? It's starting to get good, man.

Thank you, Nutty Bars, for being the oversized, peanutty Kit Kat bar. You make eating my protein so much more enjoyable.

Thank you, free pens in hotels. Oh, I'm taking you home with me. If they didn't want me to take you, then they should have put a chain on you, like at the bank.

Thank you, alligators who live on golf courses in Florida. You definitely add excitement to a rather relaxed sport.

Thank you, Thomas Nelson, for being my publisher on this project. Your commitment to excellence is second to none.

Thank you, police officers, for always having the speed trap set up right down the street from my house. I know you're just trying to protect me and give me an opportunity to pay extra money to the county again this year.

Thank you, Anne-the-editor, for making this book so much better than it ever could have been without you! Seriously, I don't think I want to write another book without you, ever.

Thank you, Chick-fil-A, for creating the most magical sauce in the world and for not charging me twenty-five cents for it like some of those other fast-food chains who will remain nameless.

Thank you, speed limit signs with both miles per hour and kilometers per hour. I always wondered what those little numbers below the big numbers on my speedometer were for. Now I know, and I still don't need to use them.

Thank you, God, for taking a guy like me and using my life to impact others. I'm so grateful for the chance to be in your service.

And thank you, reader, for making it to the end.

Stay teachable,

Matt Keller
@MatthewKeller

About the Author

Matt Keller is a people builder at his core. With more than twenty years in the people business, he is an authority on what it takes to build great teams and a great organization.

Located in Fort Myers, Florida, Matt is the founder and leader of Next Level Church, one of the fastest growing churches in America. In addition, Matt leads NextLevelCoaching.tv, an organization for pastors and church leaders, and AdvanceLeadership.tv, a coaching organization that adds value to business leaders.

His fast-paced, witty, humorous communication style will pull you in, inspire and challenge you to make the changes necessary to live up to your full potential.

Matt travels and speaks frequently working with businesses, nonprofits, and churches across the United States helping them to take their leadership and organization to the next level. For more information, go to MattKellerOnline.com.

Matt and his wife, Sarah, live in Southwest Florida with their two sons, Will and Drew. Although his love for Skittles remains, his preferred candy in this season is Reese's cups.